WHAT IS ENGLISH
TEACHING?

Open University Press

English, Language, and Education series

SELECTED TITLES IN THE SERIES

WHAT IS ENGLISH TEACHING?

Chris Davies

Open University Press
Buckingham • *Philadelphia*

Open University Press
Celtic Court
22 Ballmoor
Buckingham
MK18 1XW

and

1900 Frost Road, Suite 101
Bristol, PA 19007, USA

First Published 1996

A catalogue record of this book is available from the British Library

ISBN 0 335 19478 8 (pb)

Library of Congress Cataloging-in-Publication Data
Davies, Chris, 1948–
    What is English teaching? / by Chris Davies.
       p.   cm. — (English, language, and education series)
    Includes bibliographical references (p.   ) and index.
    ISBN 0–335–19478–8 (pb)
    1. English philology—Study and teaching.   I. Title.   II. Series.
PE65.D38   1996
428′.007—dc20   95–20672
                                                                    CIP

Typeset by Graphicraft Typesetters Ltd, Hong Kong
Printed in Great Britain by Biddles Ltd, Guildford and Kings Lynn

Contents

General editor's introduction

The 'new' version of the National Curriculum for English, after a protracted series of arguments and discussions, was finally introduced into the schools in September 1995. Under the proposals of the Dearing Report it is to remain in place for the next five years, to the end of the century in fact. In his own spirited defence of the original proposals for the English curriculum, Brian Cox, who chaired the original Working Group, claims that: 'the new English curriculum lacks vision. It reduces the curriculum to basics, many of which are clichés, and at the same time it includes . . . confusions and falsities of emphasis . . . Both pupils and teachers . . . are to some extent reduced to technicians, and the joy and wonder of the subject is lost.' (*The Battle for the English Curriculum*, Hodder and Stoughton, 1995). These are harsh judgements but they are ones that have been echoed by many commentators and teachers. Nonetheless the ingenuity of English teachers is legendary and we may hope that, over the next five years, 'vision' will not be wholly lacking in English classrooms both in England and Wales and elsewhere. Chris Davies' book is therefore timely in that, while it operates very clearly within the legal framework of the National Curriculum, it also provides that very vision that Cox finds to be sadly lacking.

It is instructive to compare Chris's account of National Curriculum English, in Chapter 3 of the present volume, with that of Brian Cox. He is obviously more able to deliver a disimpassioned judgement but he also provides a clear intellectual framework for its critique that 'the English subject area leaves the students who most need help high and dry; it allows us to believe that the issue of literacy, as the key route to intellectual success, is actually being dealt with properly in the National Curriculum. And it isn't.'

I have quoted the last sentence from Chris Davies' book directly as it is typical of the robust and direct style which informs the whole book. As we read we hear the voice of an experienced teacher and teacher educator, who is able to develop theoretical principles, notably in Chapter 2, but who also always speaks with the voice of common-sense and, even more, the sense of the classroom, seen for example, in the many examples of practical strategies that are developed throughout the book, especially in Chapter 6. There is ample material here for discussion by an English department together with fruitful ideas for the beginning as well as the experienced teacher. In a way the book is the equivalent in 1995 to one of the earliest we published in this series, Richard Knott's *The English Department in a Changing World*.

It is in a way ironic that Richard later became one of the officers of the then National Curriculum Council and that the nature of the 'changing world' of English teaching moved, under the National Curriculum discussions in which he was centrally involved, in very different directions to that envisaged in his book. If a main criticism that can be levelled against the present legal framework of the curriculum is that it is anodyne and reductionist, the present volume restores something of the balance towards the 'vision' that Cox claims is lacking.

The present day debate over the nature of English teaching has been seen by many commentators to have begun at the Anglo-American Dartmouth Seminar in 1966. The very first question that the seminar sought to answer was precisely the title of this book: What is English Teaching? After the first day's exploration of this question those of us who were present on that occasion realized that we were getting nowhere and that the question needed to be reformulated in terms of what activities go on in English classrooms. It is interesting that Chris Davies' first chapter adopts an identical strategy starting with 'some kind of picture . . . of what English teaching actually looks like, right now.' The publication of the present volume coincides with the thirtieth anniversary of Dartmouth; as Davies says, the subject 'probably won't look the same to an outsider as it did twenty, or ten, or even five years ago.'

Yet there could well remain to be discovered certain eternal verities about English teaching, features that are central to the nature of the subject and not subject to the vagaries of fashion. Davies' exploration of some of the history of the development of the subject in the immediate post-Dartmouth period, and beyond, reveals some of these and provides a working paradigm for the next five years.

Essentially the present volume provides a basis for an English teacher's work which is based upon a combination of both wisdom and experience. It listens to the voice of the classroom teacher in the way in which Brian Cox felt that the framers of new National Curriculum English singularly failed to do.

Anthony Adams

1 What actually goes on in English lessons?

This book will consider a variety of perspectives in trying to answer the question, what is English teaching? and will, in the process, twist that question into many different shapes: What does go on? How did that come about? What changes are taking place? What, ideally, ought to go on?

In order to answer those different questions, we will need to look at different kinds of evidence: instances of practice observed, changing beliefs about the subject, the demands of the outside world, the needs and characteristics of the learners themselves, and the ways in which new initiatives work in the classroom. The aim of these chapters is to accumulate a range of viewpoints which are sometimes critical of the way things are in English teaching, and hopefully provocative about the way things might be.

In thinking about where English ought to go, though, this book will not fantasize about some heroic, utopian new English. It will, instead, look carefully at the various forces that have come to make English what it currently is, and try to think how – on such a basis – it might be developed into something better. It is a question of seeing where it might be going (which is certainly part of what it is), and emphasizing aspects of that which this book will argue are both desirable *and* feasible. This book is about the reality of English teaching – where it comes from, where it is, and where it might end up, if we do our best. This book is about ways of making the best out of English, in fact.

What goes on in English lessons?

In order to achieve such an ambitious goal, it might be sensible to start with some kind of picture, however superficial and sketchy, of what English teaching actually looks like, right now. This is important, because the subject is continually developing and changing and it probably will not look the same to an outsider as it did twenty, or ten, or even five years ago. Therefore, this chapter will outline a number of different English lessons that are typical of what currently goes on in different classrooms, in different places, under the name of English.

Of course, just looking is not enough. You can not learn about an activity as complex and long term as teaching merely armed with common sense and a back-row seat in the here and now. You have got to look at other things, on a different timescale: at the different historical processes which produced the current moment; at the different kinds of pressure to which the teacher in the classroom must respond in order to do the job; at how individual lessons take their place within a whole sequence of lessons; at the physical and institutional contexts in which those lessons take place; at the particular set of individuals in the room, and the ways in which their different characteristics, needs and inclinations help determine what is going on.

But neither do any of those things mean very much if you have no mental image, no working model, for what those deeper realities amount to: the ordinary and mundane English lesson. That is where this book starts.

Ideas of English teaching

What ideas of English teaching do we hold in our minds, and where do these come from? Despite the fact that I have been professionally involved in English teaching since 1970, the first image of English teaching that comes to my mind is always the English teacher I had when I was thirteen (who told us every week that a story was like a fish – it had a head, a body and a tail) and my second image is the English teacher from the television series *Fame*, who was always an especially spiritual and profound member of a generally spiritual and profound bunch of teachers: she knew how and when to bring the best out of a disturbed adolescent, with the perfectly timed shot to the heart of Walt Whitman or Shakespeare. On the strength of many American dramas, I guess this is a kind of stereotype that goes down well in the USA, reaching its appalling apotheosis as Robin Williams in the *Dead Poets' Society*: English teaching as charisma, overstimulus, and a gushing love of literature.

The cultural models of English teaching are slightly less flashy in the UK, but no less romantic: Colin Welland as the unpretentious but honest northerner in *Kes*, with quite an eye himself for the key growth moment that finally opens up the inarticulate working-class boy, but a somewhat more bluff technique; Jean Brodie with her intense personal involvement, and her ruthless disregard for all but the most committed pupils; John Alderton with his patient and undemanding fondness for the hopeless rascals in the television series *Please Sir*. Or Scruffy McGuffy from *Grange Hill*.

But we are all, I suspect, quite hard-put to actually remember what went on in most of the lessons we sat through as children. Even if I can still recall the story-as-fish model, I could not begin to recall what the stories I wrote were actually about. In fact, I cannot recall the detail of most that went on, even if I can remember a blur of spelling tests, comprehension exercises, grammar exercises from Ronald Ridout's famous textbooks, essays, various dreary readers, *Daffodils* and Shakespeare. As my own first attempts at teaching will attest, I left school with a very incoherent sense of what English teaching was, and I suspect that is the case with most people. At any rate, if we are to build up a coherent picture of current practice, our own memories will prove to be no more helpful than Hollywood.

The latest in English teaching

All this is not to say that English teaching has completely changed in recent years, or that the changes which have occurred are of the kind one might imagine. When the politicians and pressure groups from the Right call for a return to basic and traditional English teaching, the impression is created that English teachers have been conspiring together to destroy both the English language and its literary heritage, forcing children to use non-standard forms whilst tearing up poetry anthologies. In reality, of course, the changes that have occurred in English teaching in recent years have been largely in response to radical changes to the larger education system, rather than as the outcome of some sinister conspiracy to lower standards.

A major instance of this is the way that the comprehensivization of schools in the UK during the 1960s and 1970s quite properly made English teachers re-assess subject content and subject aims. Some subject content deservedly disappeared for good (decontextualized grammar and comprehension exercises; the study of a whole substrand of English literature whose function was to celebrate the achievements of the British Empire and its attendant values; a certain kind of formal and highly artificial essay-writing). Other things with deeper roots in people's conception of the subject did begin to fade from the scene, but only temporarily as it now turns out: Shakespeare, for instance, has come back with a vengeance, and supported by an enthusiasm which strongly suggests that English teachers are not merely doing this on sufferance because the National Curriculum and its attendant testing had forced them to. They do it because they see it – and always have seen it – as integral and central to their work, along with the broader study of literary and imaginative texts, and the teaching of correct written English.

What seems to strike people most vividly who (either as beginning teachers, or as researchers) are looking at English classrooms for the first time since they left school is the dramatic change that appears to have taken place in the teaching strategies employed, rather than in the subject content taught. There appears to be considerably less teaching or lecturing from the front, whole-class question and answer, discussion, or silent individual writing than people remember. Instead, observers notice far more in the way of small group or pair work, individualized programmes of study within an overall group topic, enquiry-based, student-directed learning, and a good deal of movement and chat. It is a different, more open and engaged classroom atmosphere which observers tend to report with most amazement and, more often than not, approval.

Nonetheless, this is all impressionistic, and we should take care to ask what these surface images of English teaching might conceal, as much as focusing on what they apparently reveal. It is likely, for instance, that teachers behave differently when they are not being observed. It is certainly the case, also, that there are multiple kinds of learning intended within many English lessons, and the apparent topic of the lesson turns out to have been only the vehicle for something else. Thirdly, some activities and forms of learning in English happen too slowly for the naked eye to see, over a period of weeks rather than the minutes of a single lesson.

There are, in effect, a whole lot of reasons for saying that it is not a straightforward matter to paint a true picture of what actually goes on in English lessons. What follows, therefore, is simply a list of some of the things you might see if you put your head round the classroom door: the frequently shiny surface of English teaching beneath which this book intends to delve in various ways.

A patchwork of individual lessons

The following descriptions of English lessons were made by student teachers on the first day of their PGCE course. They were asked to jot down simply what they saw going on in a lesson they could easily recall from their previous week spent observing in schools all over the UK during September 1994. These lessons are presented in no particular or meaningful order.

1 *Language – Year 8*

The lesson begins with the teacher, through a process of question and answer with the class as a whole, helping the pupils recall that their previous lesson had dealt with the Anglo Saxons, and the early history of the English language.

Picking up from there, the teacher hands out a worksheet to every pupil containing examples of early language codes such as Celtic runes. She emphasizes the word 'code'. With the teacher's guidance, the pupils set about breaking these codes, discovering that the examples they are looking at actually stood for the names of rivers.

Then the pupils are encouraged, individually first of all, to devise their own version of a Celtic rune system in order to write their own names and addresses in code. Having warmed to this task, they are then asked to work in small groups, of four or five, and devise coded messages which they can pass to one another, as a kind of game.

2 Jane Eyre – *Year 12*

The teacher reminds the pupils that the lesson is to take the form of a seminar on *Jane Eyre*. A number of pupils then take turns to read out a paper they have prepared on the various different homes that Jane Eyre goes into, and the way her spiritual and intellectual growth can be seen as being symbolized by these houses.

At the end of each paper, all the pupils engage in a short discussion about the points that were made. Occasionally, the teacher steps in to guide the discussion, pointing out important questions and issues which a particular paper raises. The teacher makes a point of encouraging various pupils to express their own views.

As the lesson progresses, the pupils talk and argue increasingly with each other, and the teacher intervenes only occasionally to keep things moving along.

3 Shape poetry – Year 8

The teacher writes the words 'the slippery slimy snooty snake' in the shape of a snake on the blackboard. After a few comments from the pupils, revealing that they grasp the concept of a shape poem, they set about producing their own examples. They write about things such as ghosts, animals and bicycles, each producing their own example, but chatting to their neighbour and showing each other what they are producing as they go along.

The teacher encourages the pupils to improve on their first attempts by thinking about what words will work best in their shape poems. They are encouraged to ignore normal grammatical rules, and are reminded of devices such as alliteration, assonance and onomatopoeia, which they pick up and use with enthusiasm.

They work busily and productively throughout the lesson.

4 Aliens story – Year 7

The pupils listen to a story read by the teacher about aliens, and then split into groups in order to carry out a variety of tasks.

First they are asked to draw their own imaginary alien. Then they must write a letter describing themselves and their own world in general to this alien.

The pupils work in fairly large groups – average eight per group – and appear to discuss their ideas with each other throughout the process.

5 Future fiction – Year 7

The teacher unlocks the door and lets 25 young people into a room. They talk to each other and jostle one another as they enter. The teacher tells them to 'Settle down' and looks at one laughing boy in particular and says 'Enough'.

Then he begins talking – about the future – a fantasy future in which different pupils themselves star in unlikely roles. He looks from one pupil to another weaving them all into his rambling story. They all laugh a lot. The teacher tells his tale like an actor playing to an audience – funny voices are spoken.

Eventually he stops talking and tells the young people to write their own possible future, using dialogue as the main device.

6 *Autobiography – Year 9*

Pupils sitting at tables in groups of six, with the teacher moving amongst the groups. The teacher gets the pupils to continue writing their personal birth experiences, a task which had been begun in the previous lesson and is now being completed.

Then she selects some of the pieces and the pupils read them to the class. Comments are passed by teacher and pupils about the style of writing, which leads on to a discussion of what autobiography is.

After much discussion – in groups, with the teacher sitting at her desk – the teacher moves the topic onto the pupils' first memories. After allowing a period of time for group discussion about group memories, the teacher asks the pupils to write down their ideas. As their work proceeds, the teacher gets individual pupils to come to her desk with their work, which she discusses in terms of grammar, punctuation, etc.

7 *Car poem – Year 7*

First the pupils individually silently read a short poem about a car. Then the class divides into small groups and sets about locating American English words in the poem, as well as any phrases in general which seem peculiar to them as British English speakers. This leads to about 10 minutes of debate and analysis.

Then the class gets back together, and the teacher reads the poem out loud, asking the pupils to 'beep' when an American word appears. They do this with enthusiasm.

Subsequently, the teacher leads a whole-class discussion, in which pupils consider other kinds of outside influence on language, such as the cinema, TV and newspapers.

8 The Big Easy – *Year 10*

The teacher, sitting beside a TV and VCR shows segments of the film *The Big Easy*, and leads the pupils – who are sitting in a semi-circle around the TV – in a critical discussion about film techniques.

From time to time, the teacher freezes the image, and the pupils take note of camera positions, etc. At the same time, he leads the pupils in discussion of narrative, getting them to comment on the central characters, and the way the story is being built up. The pupils take notes and respond freely.

Then the teacher focuses on one scene in particular, and the pupils clear space so that they can have a go at standing in the same positions as the actors in the film, and work out where the camera would be.

Finally, the pupils tell each other about the various detective stories they were asked to read previously, for reporting back in this lesson.

9 *Persuasive writing – Year 9*

All the class are crowded round the TV screen watching a black-and-white edition of Brutus's speech following the death of Caesar. After ten minutes, the pupils return to their desks, some with their backs to the teacher, and take up listening poses.

The teacher then starts to ask how the speaker on the film gained the support of the audience; the teacher himself is sitting on his desk and leaning enthusiastically forward towards his pupils.

Everyone is encouraged to analyse the speech and then a different example of persuasive text, in order to find clues about the techniques being used. A photocopy of something called a *Parents' Guide to Nintendo Games* is considered, leaving the pupils with a rather sinister view of those who promote such games.

10 To Kill a Mockingbird – *Year 11*

The lesson starts in an unexpected manner, because one pupil raises a difficulty she is experiencing with a piece of work which the teacher had previously set for them. She is soon vigorously supported by several other pupils, so that the teacher has no choice but to abandon his original plan for a while.

The pupils had been asked to describe the trial scene in *To Kill a Mockingbird* from a personal viewpoint, writing (a) as a white spectator and (b) as a black spectator. The pupils – in response to the teacher's probing – explain that whilst they can understand the factual content, they have difficulty in grasping the empathy element of the task.

The teacher elicits a fairly comprehensive factual recall of the scene, and then tries to lead the pupils towards the required viewpoint by helping them think about the experience of specific characters, asking questions such as 'Where was Scout while this was going on?' and 'Why did she have to sit there?'

The teacher reminds pupils of quotations from the book, asking them why they think particular characters said these things.

This leads into a more general reminder of the issues the teacher wants the pupils to consider: what was special about Scout and Jem's upbringing, and about Atticus as a father? What were the prevailing conditions of the time? Issues of fear and envy, and Atticus's own integrity are emphasized.

The teacher finally moves on to the planned lesson, in which the pupils watch a video about the deep south of the USA. The class sit around the TV, and the teacher stops and starts the video in order to emphasize certain crucial points.

Other lessons

The final five lessons will be summarized very briefly:

11 The exploration of male/female stereotypes in advertising through the discussion and analysis of adverts in small groups (Year 9).

12 The discussion and analysis of love poetry in small groups (Year 11).

13 A different lesson, in a different school, on *To Kill a Mockingbird*, in which the pupils (in small groups) explore their thoughts about one particular

character, Boo Radley, by imagining themselves in that character's role (Year 10).

14 The application of technical literary critical terms (pathos, stichomythia) to the script and video of an Alan Bennett monologue, leading to a discussion of the characterization (Year 12).

15 An introduction to the study of *Tess of the D'Urbevilles* for an A-level group, focusing on the historical and geographical context from which Hardy wrote the book (Year 12).

On the basis of this small sample of 15 lessons, one does get the impression that studying English in the secondary school looks quite enjoyable. It is likely, of course, that these students tended not to choose the duller (to the eyes of a novice), bread-and-butter lessons in which much useful learning might actually have gone on. Still, we can use this selection to formulate a few tentative hypotheses about English teaching, which might at least point in the direction of further fruitful enquiry.

For instance:

- English teachers try to make their lessons varied and active for the pupils: Pupils work as a whole class, in pairs, in small groups and individually; they play games, break codes and devise codes, draw pictures of aliens, make beeping noises, simulate film-making, run seminars and write curvy poems. Teachers lecture, tell stories, make jokes, quietly encourage, sit on their desks and chat to the whole class, walk round the room and nudge groups of pupils into action, sit at their desks and work with individuals.

- The subject-matter of English tends to be fairly abstract and non-instrumental: Pupils learn about the nature of language, the techniques used by professional authors and by media professionals, the internal dynamics of fictional events and representations, and the practice of imaginative/creative/expressive writing.

- It is not easy to identify a single overriding learning aim for a particular English lesson: Pupils study poems in order to develop their oral skills or their awareness of the processes of language change; pupils write science fiction in order to develop their descriptive skills, or their ability to handle the conventions of dialogue; pupils write autobiography in order to provide a context for developing their literacy skills; pupils study Shakespeare in order to learn about the persuasive techniques of modern media, or they study the persuasive techniques of modern media in order to learn about Shakespeare, or both.

- Whatever the learning aim, English teaching predominantly involves the study or production of texts of an imaginative/creative/expressive kind: the only occasions in these 15 examples when English shows any sign of addressing all the other ways that language matters to us in the world – as learners, workers, citizens, intimates, travellers, and consumers – is in the lesson on advertising, and the examination of a *Parents' Guide to Nintendo*

Games, although obviously a lot of English teachers would claim that literature is the best way of dealing with *all* those aspects of our lives.

There are other notable gaps which ought to be mentioned. For example, there is only one instance here of an English teacher actually working on what the outside world quite possibly considers the most important task of English teaching: helping children to write accurately. This is either because (a) English teachers do not often actually teach basic literacy skills directly or overtly, preferring as a rule to embed such learning within other kinds of learning, in the context of other activities; or (b) it is because English teachers simply do not teach much in the way of basic literacy skills at all. The truth is probably varied, but I trust the evidence of these 15 examples enough to stick with the cautious hypothesis that maybe not a lot of direct teaching of literacy skills goes on in secondary English classrooms.

On the other hand, I know perfectly well that certain frequently encountered aspects of English teaching are underrepresented here. Shakespeare, for one; an absence which can probably be explained by the fact that these observations occurred in September, and it is likely that exam-minded teachers choose to teach Shakespeare later in the year. There are inevitably many other false impressions given by that list, but that is the whole point really: one aim of this list was to demonstrate how varied and unpredictable (at least to outsiders) English teaching appears to be, and much more complex than our own common sense knowledge of the world might make us expect.

The shape of this book

English teaching is, like any professional activity, internally coherent, rational and comprehensible. That must be the case – it keeps on carrying on in a more or less recognizable form, despite strong pressures to change, and its many and varied practitioners usually understand what they have to say to each other about what they do. It is the aim of the following chapters to open up the internal logic and reasoning underlying English teaching, and on the basis of that, to begin to think about where those things might lead in the future. As a means of doing so (and I acknowledge that there could be a thousand other ways of trying this), I have arranged the chapters as following:

Chapters 2 to 4 are all my own work, and are not necessarily the views of the other contributors to this book. First, Chapter 2 looks at English teachers' beliefs about English teaching, because these are both deeply rooted and highly influential on what actually goes on. But then, so is the National Curriculum, the development of which in terms of the English subject area Chapter 3 will investigate and interpret in detail. On the basis of the rather unenthusiastic conclusions drawn from this, Chapter 4 then explores the scope for developing a more forward-looking English curriculum, which attempts to address the needs and realities of the world our young people actually inhabit.

Chapter 5, by Peter Benton, looks in fascinating detail at certain aspects of that world. Based on research which he is still in the process of carrying out, Peter presents a picture of the cultural world of young people in the UK which has immense implications for how a responsive and contemporary English teaching might engage with the real lives and experiences of learners.

In Chapter 6, Christine Lawson explains both the development and current nature of the principles underlying her work in the classroom. This chapter crucially emphasizes the centrality of English teaching strategies in any thinking about the nature of the subject today. Then, in Chapter 7, Kathy Oxtoby skilfully brings together the different perspectives which have helped her, as a new English teacher, to make sense of the various things that she might do as an English teacher, and in particular those things which might best address the needs of the learners themselves.

Chapter 8, a summary of the implications of this book, will have to speak for itself when the time comes, because I am not sure if I like the idea of summing up the summary of what the book has said before the book has even said it!

I hope you enjoy reading it all.

2 English teachers' beliefs about English teaching

> The English teachers held strong ideological commitments and beliefs, central to which were a number of truths which were taken to be self-evident, but which were essentially unprovable. They held that pupils could and would enter a fuller, freer life through writing, discussing their own and other people's writing, and by the act of making the kind of judgements which are made by writers of fiction, plays and poetry. These truths were the badges of the faithful . . .
>
> (Brooks, 1983: 39)

It does seem to be the case that a strong commitment to certain shared values and beliefs is more or less part of an English teacher's job description. The precise nature of these values and beliefs is probably in a constant state of development and change, but the value-driven nature of actually being an English teacher does appear to be a striking, and deeply rooted, aspect of the role. In this respect, Caroline St. John-Brooks' description of English teachers' beliefs as 'the badges of the faithful' nicely captures the two key elements of: (a) English teachers' profound convictions about the purposes of their work; and (b) the important role these beliefs play in establishing, and expressing, the individual and group identities of English teachers.

This chapter looks at the kinds of values and beliefs English teachers hold in relation to their subject, at how these are transmitted and sustained within the profession, and at how they develop and change. Of course, it might seem irrelevant to think in such terms at all any more, given the fact that the degree of teacher control over the curriculum has been considerably reduced in the UK, as in other countries, in the interests of guaranteeing certain agreed learning goals for all students. Chapter 3 will consider some of the difficulties which do emerge when that central government goes so far as to undermine teachers' sense of professional control and involvement in their teaching, but in general, despite the real reduction that has occurred in recent years to teachers' freedom to determine their own curriculum, it is nonetheless the case that a centralized curriculum still allows teachers to play a significant part, along with central policymakers, in deciding what should be learnt, and how that should be learnt.

At any rate, in order to understand the aims for the subject which the National Curriculum is attempting to establish, we need to look at the sort of aims which underpinned thinking about the subject in the years leading up to present developments. That thinking was done mainly, in those relatively free and easy times, by the teachers themselves, so this chapter therefore concentrates mainly on what they had to say about the subject.

Paradigms, philosophies, recipes and aims

There are a number of terms one might use to describe the values and beliefs that people hold about a shared enterprise such as English teaching. 'Aims' is probably the most useful overall term, because that does very effectively encompass both what people feel needs to be *done* in the classroom, as well as the ideals to which people aspire in selecting particular actions. To a certain extent, talking about one's educational aims is a slightly less portentous way of talking about one's educational philosophy: whether talking about subject aims or subject philosophy, we are referring to the things that teachers wish to state, to the rest of the world, about their intentions, beliefs and aspirations concerning the work they do.

Stephen Ball and Colin Lacey, in their study of subject subcultures, offer a further refinement on notions such as aims or philosophy by identifying two more specific, and distinctive, terms, 'subject paradigm' and 'subject pedagogy':

> . . . subject paradigm refers to the views of English as a subject held by English teachers in terms of the appropriate content. . . . subject pedagogy refers to the system of ideas and procedures for the organisation of learning in the classroom under specific institutional conditions, that is appropriate method rather than appropriate content.
>
> (Ball and Lacey, 1994)

This is obviously a helpful and important distinction, as it is certainly the case that English teachers have convictions about the *ways in which* they teach that are as deep as their convictions about *what* they ought to teach. The term 'subject pedagogy' stands for the complex array of technical skills which English teachers deploy in making the chosen content (now increasingly determined by policymakers rather than teachers) learnable: perhaps this term is what best represents English teachers' professional craft knowledge.

The distinction is particularly important because it offers a sort of conceptual lever for pulling apart what English teachers often tend to conflate: the subject content to be learned and the activities selected to achieve that learning. Such a conflation tends to result in a slightly bewildering looseness about aims.

English teachers have often tended to be quite unfocused in the way they define their aims. That is to say, they often view what goes on in their classrooms in a very inclusive way, so that everything that happens in a lesson is counted as contributing to students' learning. For instance, in a lesson which is ostensibly intended to help the students understand the first scene of *Romeo and Juliet* through the use of whole-class discussion, small group work, computers, and media study (in order to produce a tabloid account of the street brawl in 'The Verona Chronicle'), a teacher (or student) might identify the learning which happened as (a) about Shakespeare, (b) about newspapers, (c) about oral skills, and so on. In the end it, becomes difficult to distinguish what was *learnt*, from what was *done*.

All this seems fair enough, and in some ways desirable, but if learning is in everything then it might sometimes be difficult to know whether or not it happened. There is some value in prioritizing – for one thing, it makes it easier to get a fix on the outcomes of the teaching process. If the broad content, the specific learning aims, and the teaching strategies all flow into one grand holistic soup, one ends up with the kind of long-term strategy – a sort of hope, really – that all these different learning events will just somehow build up into some constructive purpose inside the learners over time.

The terms 'subject paradigm' and 'subject pedagogy' point, ultimately, to the need for English teachers to be analytical about what they do, at least from time to time. There is, for instance, a great deal to be said for being clear about what learning ought to be achieved at any one time, in a deliberate and targeted way, and in order to do that it is necessary to break down and see the differences between *what* one wants children to learn, the *material* you will use to help them learn that, and the *teaching strategies* you will deploy to help that material bring about that learning.

As the philosophical assertions which follow suggest, English teachers have often preferred deep conviction to cool analysis. This is not to suggest that English teachers are irrational, but there has often in the past of English teaching been a considerable resistance to anything smacking too much of the instrumental, the oversystematic, to anything that takes the shine off the loftier aspirations which they espouse. And unless one accepts the need for a more analytical approach, there is a real danger that the English subject paradigm (the way its aims, content, purpose, boundaries, etc. are formulated) might just turn out to be more in the interests of the English teachers themselves – imbuing familiar and comfortable practices, knowledge and beliefs with a gratifying sense of legitimacy – than of the actual students.

Of course, it is very difficult to be truly analytical about things that are a very close and normal part of one's life. In this respect, the term 'recipe' as used by the sociologist Alfred Schutz back in the 1930s is quite helpful. In his article 'The Stranger', Schutz helps us think about the ways in which particular social groups share values, meanings, habits and rules about their particular social world through the device of exploring what it is that a *stranger* to that world must understand in order to make sense of it. By stranger, he means sociologist, the person whose task in relation to this world *is* to be analytical, rather than active. This is a crucial distinction, because 'the actor within the social world, however, experiences it primarily as a field of his actual and possible acts and only secondarily as an object of his thinking' (Schutz, 1971).

This actor *within* a particular social group (and I am obviously suggesting that English teachers do indeed constitute such a social group) works 'within a ready-made standardized scheme' of the 'valuations, institutions, and systems of orientation and guidance' of the group. This standardized scheme – which Schutz also talks of in terms of 'thinking-as-usual' and the 'of-course' assumptions of a particular social group – provides:

> a knowledge of trustworthy *recipes* for interpreting the social world and for hand-ling things and men in order to obtain the best results in every situation with a minimum of effort by avoiding undesirable consequences. The recipe works, on the one hand, as a precept for actions and thus serves as a scheme of expression: whoever wants to obtain a certain result has to proceed as indicated by the recipe provided for that purpose. On the other hand, the recipe serves as a scheme of interpretation: whoever proceeds as indicated by a specific recipe is supposed to intend the correlated results. Thus it is the function of the cultural pattern to eliminate troublesome enquiries by offering ready-made directions for use, to replace truth hard to attain by comfortable truisms, and to substitute the self-explanatory for the questionable.
>
> (Schutz, 1971)

The whole function of these recipes, as Schutz describes them, is to enable the activities of the social group to proceed effectively and smoothly, and also to make the activities of the group feel worthwhile and even special. In order for that to happen, one must both know what to do, and how to talk about it, in ways that will be shared, understood and approved by the other members of the group. As far as those students might be concerned, these recipes may or may not be entirely effective in the way they meet all the English-learning needs that they might have (the recipes obviously cannot be entirely useless, because in that case the activities of the social group of English teachers would grind to a halt), but seeing them as recipes also raises the possibility that they need not necessarily be entirely logical, coherent or consistent with the de-mands these learners must satisfy during their lives as users of English.

This sounds hostile, but really it is just an attempt to find a way of standing *outside* English teaching for a moment. Given the complex – sometimes bewil-dering – breadth of its interests, it is obviously important that everyone con-cerned with its activities (teachers, students, parents, policymakers) are able to question and probe beneath the surprisingly tough surface of convictions with which it protects its aims and ideals. It is particularly important, of course, that those about to join (and be socialized into the norms of) the particular social group of English teachers are able to question the deep-rooted certainties of the experienced practitioners from whom they will largely learn. It is in such a questioning attitude that one should think about the kinds of aims and conviction which follow.

English teachers' Statements of Aims

One source of evidence about deep-rooted beliefs is the 'Statement of Aims' which individual subject departments in schools produced for public consumption (i.e. for parents, governors and HMI) in a period of increased accountability during the late 1970s and early 1980s. The following extracts – in this case, all coming from a number of such produced by secondary English departments in the comprehensive schools of one Local Education Authority during this period – reveal a lot about how English teachers at that moment in the subject's history chose, or felt obliged, to represent themselves and their work to the outside world and to each other at that time (when a National Curriculum was more or less unimagined). Obviously, when looking at these kinds of statements, one might be tempted to suspect that people do not necessarily *believe* the things they say professionally and publicly, but sincerity is not really the point here. These statements are most interesting when one views them as recipes for doing the job and, as Schutz points out above, such recipes are intended both as guidance for action, and as a source of ready-made explanations and justifications for those actions which can be shared and recognized by all members of the social group. They must, in effect, sound good without being too complex and problematic.

On the basis of this evidence about teachers' views about the aims and content of English, they seem to be pretty skilful at writing their recipes. Especially skilful in this respect, is the way these statements achieve the sensation of coherence without committing themselves to much in the way of curriculum detail: a central theme in these statements is the notion of freedom from *prescription, specificity* or (a neat little rhetorical jink) *rigidity*.

> The department has developed into an informal and flexible team, with shared aims but without the imposition of narrowly prescriptive methods or approaches. Individuality and variety of approach are the keynotes and regular departmental discussion on a wide variety of topics related to the teaching of English ensures that individuality does not become eccentricity.
>
> Within this atmosphere, we all felt that we wished to avoid a detailed list of objectives which could easily come to restrict our individual approaches.
>
> (School 3)

This theme is repeated in virtually every document, nearly always in relation to claims about the special way in which the subject of English, or rather the teachers of English themselves if left to get on with it, can develop the whole child:

> We want our pupils to be aware of themselves and others in as wide a context as possible, both spatial and temporal; we want them to think, feel and communicate in ways of value to themselves and the community; we want them to 'follow an imaginative course, based upon the needs of adolescents in contemporary society, which will develop their intellectual, aesthetic and spiritual resources'. No attempt

will be made to detail rigid schemes of work for the achievement of this aim. Every teacher is different; every class is different.

(School 4)

Our general aims are: (1) the development of the personality through greater self-knowledge and through the extension of horizons by perception of the experiences, actual or imaginative, of others; . . . English is not a subject with a set syllabus of materials to be used or studied, and one of the beauties of the subject is the freedom it provides for teacher to use materials which inspire him or which inspire a particular set of pupils.

(School 5)

It is one of the joyous labours of an English teacher to devise an infinite variety of stimulating ideas and exercises . . .

(School 6)

That theme is justified by another central theme: the exceptional character of English as a subject (which naturally permits a certain freedom from constraint):

Although we run the risk of exaggerating our significance, there is little doubt that as English teachers we do occupy a unique position. To begin with, we are teaching a subject that is of crucial importance in our pupils' lives in a way that many other subjects are not.

(School 1)

The nature of that unique position is often described by the teachers in terms that stretch the role of English outside its own self-evident subject content (i.e. literacy, oracy and literature):

English, more than perhaps any other subject, can have an extremely humanising effect and emphasis on the academic should not be to the detriment of enlarging the personality and developing an awareness of the world outside the classroom.

(School 2)

The following claims are logically also way beyond the scope of a mere English teacher, although clearly some kind of underlying relationship between subject content and intended outcomes is implied here:

As teachers of English, we consider it our duty:
(a) to enrich the child's experience and to broaden his [sic] horizons through literature;
(b) to stimulate his [sic] imagination;
(c) to awaken his [sic] sensitivity to human emotions;
(d) to help him [sic] think for himself [sic] and to be able to confront the pressure of the mass media;
(e) to develop in the child a sense of tolerance and understanding;
(f) to develop a sense of social awareness;
(g) to realise his [sic] full potential in the broad field entitled 'English'.

(School 7)

Such claims are, of course (as Caroline St. John Brooks suggests), an act of faith: the logic of the implied connections between the study of literature, the stimulation of the imagination, and the awakening of the young person's sensitivity to human emotions is neither argued nor arguable. If you join this social group, it seems, you are left with no option but to accept the truth of this. Ball and Lacey's article (referred to above) nicely illustrates this process in action, when they ask the Head of English whose department they were observing whether all the members of his department share his view of the subject. He replies:

'Yes. Most of the members of the department; the majority of the department have been appointed in fact since I've been Head of the department and this is one of the things that I'm looking for when I'm wondering whether somebody's going to fit in. . . . I mean if somebody came to my department and wanted to teach formal grammar all of the time, or wanted to do funny exercises from a course book, and thought that this was the way to improve language work. Or wanted to use those 'English in Use' things. I think obviously they wouldn't fit in. But you find that out at interview.'

(Ball and Lacey, 1994: 240, 242)

As that comment shows, it is not just any old idiosyncratic set of beliefs that an aspiring member of this department needs to hold in order to gain admission. Clearly this Head of department requires a certain sort of non-instrumental, flexible commitment to a personal-development-through-literature model of English, something which in fact appears over and over in these English Department Statements of Aims:

Aims
To develop a personal response to literature and enjoyment of literature as a way of liberating the imagination and exploring experience.

(School 8)

Aims
To foster enjoyment in reading. To provide access to as much good literature as possible, presenting in such a way that it may:

(a) provoke and develop spiritual and imaginative response
(b) extend awareness of others and other ideas
(c) increase self-awareness and sensitivity

(School 9)

References to language skills seem pretty half-hearted in comparison:

Aims
To develop skills of *communication*, including attention to the basic skills of spelling, punctuation, grammar; *creativity*, including a sense of curiosity; and *criticism*, including a sense of literary awareness.

Such an emphasis also came out very strongly in the comprehensive school English department which Caroline St. John Brooks studied at around the same time that all the above statements were written, providing a more three-dimensional confirmation of the impressions created by these Statements of Aims. She encountered a group of English teachers who 'whilst not denying the importance of literacy skills, consider them as a means to an end, the end being a fuller and freer, more critical and more constructive, inner life for their students. This, they believe, can best be achieved in dialogue with the minds of others, through the medium of literature'. (Brooks, 1980: 304). She describes one teacher in particular as being 'committed to the emotional education of his students, . . . of a very particular kind – a serious commitment to self-understanding through literature' (Brooks, 1980: 286). She also identified a negative aspect to that commitment, in the way that the teachers found it hard not to prefer those more academic children who could make sense of and respond to their particular preoccupations with demanding literary material and concepts. Such a systematic differentiation is more crudely expressed in this last extract from another school department's policy document:

> As a department we feel that there are some well-known works and types of literature with which at least the more able of our pupils should, at some stage, become acquainted.
>
> (School 10)

This is an abiding dilemma for English teachers – do you accept different aspirations for different students, as the above school has done, or do you risk failure for some by aspiring for the same high-level learning for all? The teachers in Caroline St. John Brooks' study aimed for the latter, more idealistic option, and encountered problems – not least because the students and the teachers did not share the same recipes for their learning. She characterizes this gap in terms of a 'romanticist' and 'rationalist' divide, with the teachers adopting the romanticist position:

> From the rationalist perspective, education is training for work, and schools are responsible for equipping children with skills to sell in the market-place. Romanticism, on the other hand, sees education as personal development. So far as English is concerned, conflict can arise between those who see the subject in terms of acquisition of literacy skills (spelling, grammar, letter-writing) which are needed to pass examinations and get a job, and English teachers committed to what they see as the nurture of human qualities vital to personal and expressive development.

Brooks makes it clear that the teachers' romanticist emphasis on personal and expressive development left many students high and dry, and feeling short-changed:

> . . . interviews with pupils revealed that many lower-band children, who were nearly all working class, thought the English teachers should spend more time on teaching them basic skills . . .

Brooks argues that:

> without carefully constructed bridges between students' everyday lives and the world of the English lesson [the kind of teaching that the English teachers in this school were so strongly committed to was] most likely to find a worthwhile response in those students who are already confident in their judgements, who are used to seeing their personal experience as significant. In short: the middle class.
>
> (Brooks, 1983)

Where do philosophical positions such as these actually come from? The intensity with which Brooks' English teachers describe their beliefs makes it appear as if they had been forged out of their own personal philosophies, but the evidence of history suggests otherwise. The English teachers described here belong squarely in a tradition which can be tracked back to Matthew Arnold, and which found its apotheosis in the work of F.R. Leavis. Whilst others have already covered this history in more than adequate detail (notably in Mathieson, 1975), it is worth briefly considering here the central role played in the development of subject recipes by those subject gurus whose task it was to provide the permanent textual authority behind the more transient and fragmentary subject recipes which turn up in curriculum documents.

In particular, it is helpful to look at one or two of the individuals who, on the evidence of the way their ideas echo on down through the years in curriculum documents, do seem to have been influential on these ways of thinking. During the 1960s, these figures formulated and consolidated views of English teaching which fertilized the early professional development of those people who went on to be Heads of English departments in the 1970s and 1980s. Prime candidates in this respect must be David Holbrook and John Dixon, whose most well-known texts (*English for Maturity* by Holbrook and *Growth through English* by Dixon) encompass the period, a time in which a new kind of secondary English was being forged to meet the needs of CSE and the beginnings of comprehensivization.

Both Holbrook and Dixon share a passionate and confident belief that English teaching is centrally concerned with literature, although Holbrook's essentially Leavisite vision is slightly more grand, or grandiose, in the way it aspires to engage with the cultural health of the whole nation through English teaching. Holbrook re-applied a vision from university education to the very different context of the secondary modern schools where non-academic children were educated. It was, in effect, quite an audacious undertaking, encouraging English literature graduates to teach in secondary modern schools, where they would find 'the three quarters of the population on the quality of whose lives the fibre of England as a nation depends' (Holbrook, 1961: 6–7). Holbrook's vision reads as genuine democratic idealism, although such a concern for the moral development of the working classes can also be located within a less-appealing tradition in which the middle classes have tried to deploy the resources within their control – such as the experience of high culture – in order to keep the working classes quiet. George Sampson somewhat gave the game away in *English for the English* when he suggested:

> Deny to working-class children any common share in the immaterial, and presently they will grow into the men who demand with menaces a communism of the material.

(Sampson, 1925)

Holbrook, though, offered a vision of profound importance to English teachers, in suggesting that it was they alone who could do such work, by providing the experience of certain kinds texts and discourses – imaginative, symbolic, concerned with human emotions and life's fundamental experiences, and essentially of a literary nature. English, he explained, with the absolute conviction of the true guru, 'must be at the centre of all education'.

Dixon's prescriptions six years later in *Growth through English* – however much they reflect the rapid cultural and educational changes which took place during that time in the UK – express the same fundamental values: an absolute conviction about the primacy of the English teacher's role in the education of the full social range of young people, and an utter confidence in the power of the same broad notion of texts and discourses. The 1960s were in full flower, though, and it was no longer fashionable to talk in terms of the health and fibre of the nation – Dixon prefers to emphasize the *individual* child. Neither is Dixon as keen as Holbrook was on finding 'touchstone' texts; he prefers to encourage students' own uses of the symbolic, imaginative language that embodies what Holbrook values in literary texts. Underlying Dixon's argument (which is also the case in some of Holbrook's writing) there is an invocation of something that sounds psychological, assigning to these claims a certain gloss of scientific validity:

> In English, pupils meet to share their encounters with life, and to do this effectively they move freely between dialogue and monologue – between talk, drama and writing; and literature, by bringing new voices into the classroom, adds to the store of shared experience. Each pupil takes from the store what he [*sic* here and to the end of quote] can and what he needs. In so doing he learns to use language to build his own representational world and to make this fit reality as he experiences it. . . . In ordering and composing situations that in some way symbolize life as we know it, we bring order and composure to our inner selves. When a pupil is steeped in language in operation we expect, as he matures, a conceptualising of his earlier awareness of language, and with this perhaps new insight into himself (as creator of his own world).

(Dixon, 1967: 13)

The impression of science was not the only way in which Dixon manages to establish his particular vision of the subject. He also makes great play throughout *Growth through English* of the fact that the ideas and formulations he offers are very much the product of a collaborative effort (at a transatlantic conference of English teachers in 1966), thus formulating recipes which arrive in the world symbolically authenticated by representatives of the full English teachers' social group.

But perhaps Dixon's most useful contribution to the way in which English teachers themselves went on to formulate their ideas about their work was his emphasis on a 'unitary' rather than a 'fragmented' approach to the subject. In more recent years, the term used would probably have been 'holistic' – he is insistent that all the activities of English (Dixon cites four: composition, language, literature, poetry) should flow together. Given the imprecision of these four categories of English study, it is not surprising that they do turn out to be quite easily synthesized, but that is not really the point. In advocating this 'unitary' approach, Dixon states a principle which many subsequent Heads of English appear to have enthusiastically adopted in their statements of belief and intent:

> If in the course of reading some poems with a class, the teacher sees possibilities for acting, or if in the accompanying talk students are so seized with the topic that they want to write, then a unitary approach permits the flow from a prepared activity to one relatively unforeseen. Lessons become less preformulated. This is not to reject pre-planning and system: on the contrary, a teacher who is planning flexibly needs to consider beforehand many possible avenues that his students may discover in the course of a lesson, so that whichever catches their enthusiasm is aware of its possibilities. The more active the part pupils are given, the more difficult to predict all that they will find and uncover: thus the need for a flexible teaching strategy rather than rigid lesson plans . . .
>
> (Dixon, 1967: 33)

This combined emphasis upon enthusiasm and flexibility appears highly attractive, and is evidently fully in tune with those aspects of this broad philosophy that were already in place in Holbrook's account, in that this view of what goes on in English lessons involves the learner's whole being, rather than specific (or 'fragmented') bits of learning. The English teacher is presented as someone who orchestrates, stimulates and personally engages in this ongoing interaction between experience and language which is presumed to be constantly happening in English classrooms. Of course, this does also reflect the problem previously raised in this chapter about evading the responsibility for identifying clear and specific learning aims, the achievement of which might actually be monitored and assessed.

There are other figures – people like Harold Rosen, James Britton, Douglas Barnes – who wrote with great creativity and originality about English teaching, and whose influence eventually worked its way into the thinking of English teachers. But such influence was not achieved quickly, especially when it entailed a more rigorous formulation of subject recipes. One has only to consider the time it took for Barnes' compelling arguments concerning the relationship between talk and learning, or Britton's challenging ideas about writing, to gain general acceptance in order to suspect that an important criterion of subject recipes is *comfortable fit*.

At the same time, those recipes accrete a variety of accommodations to new realities – changes in the popular culture, changes in academic fashion, changes in educational structures and policies, and simply changes in time (what once was new must be renewed on a fairly regular basis) – which sometimes trickle and sometimes burst through into the current ways of thinking, and do create their own valuable moments of discomfort and disorientation. The fact is that, during the period between the time at the end of the 1970s when the Statements of Aims quoted above were written, and the time a decade later when the National Curriculum was introduced in the UK, significant changes *were* beginning to take place in the English curriculum, and in the ways in which teachers (some, at least) viewed their work.

Changing English

A variety of factors eventually combined to shift the paradigm of English studies during the early 1980s. Various dimensions of change played a part in this, such as the following: the explosion of a new vigorous youth-oriented popular culture in the 1960s; the growth and consolidation of TV as the central form of mass communication; the move to comprehensivization in schools; social, political and intellectual revolutions in Europe and USA; and new waves of social and cultural theory within higher education in Europe and USA. Some of these influences directly changed secondary teaching, some came up through progressive initiatives in primary education, and some worked their way down from the field of higher education, which itself was trying to come to terms with changes in the outside world. In the case of English it seemed that something quite different and dramatic was finally bursting into bloom during the early 1980s (it had taken a while – the seeds had been steadily blowing over from France for twenty years). Raymond Williams, talking specifically about this crisis in terms of Cambridge University English described the process by which subject recipes or paradigms in general, and those for English in particular change, thus:

> such paradigms are never simply abandoned. Rather they accumulate anomalies until there is eventually a breaking point, and attempts are made to shift and replace the fundamental hypothesis, its definitions and what are by this stage the established professional standards and methods of enquiry. That evidently is a moment of crisis.

(Williams, 1983: 192)

The crisis described by Williams threatened for a while to change English studies in higher education quite violently. A few undergraduate courses were significantly rewritten, introducing the study of literary theory, which was not the same as literary criticism (in some respects literary theory questioned the whole validity of literary criticism as an activity), and in some quarters the Leavisite tradition, characterized as *liberal humanist*, became severely discredited, in favour of a range of (sometimes wildly differing) positions which included structuralism, post-structuralism, psychoanalytic criticism and Marxist criticism.

What these had in common was a concern for the way that cultural forms and texts (including, among other things, literature) were the product of forces other than the singular inspiration of their authors. If cultural forms and texts expressed more complex social/political/psychological processes than their actual authors were aware of, it followed that the established focus, within the existing traditions of English literary study, on the individual writer as creator of texts and source of insights no longer sufficed. Catherine Belsey was quite clear about the kind of change that was taking place:

> the notion of a text which tells a (or the) truth, as perceived by an individual subject (the author), whose insights are the source of the text's single and authoritative meaning, is not only untenable but literally unthinkable, because the framework which supported it, a framework of assumptions and discourses, ways of thinking and talking, no longer stands.
>
> (Belsey, 1980)

Elsewhere, Belsey spoke of treating English 'as a site of struggle', in order to generate a new critical discourse. It is evident from what is now a very substantial literature advocating, analysing, and applying, literary theory that this indeed is precisely what happened. As far as secondary teaching is concerned, though, the often complex intricacies are less relevant than the broader acts of iconoclasm which cleared space for such work in the first place. It is out of texts such as Terry Eagleton's *Literary Theory: an introduction* (which quickly became a best seller at undergraduate level) that the new slogans came that threatened the stability of existing subject recipes:

> Any belief that the study of literature is the study of a stable, well-definable entity, as entomology is the study of insects, can be abandoned as a chimera. Some kinds of fiction are literature and some are not; some literature is fictional and some is not; some literature is verbally self-regarding, while some highly-wrought rhetoric is not literature. Literature, in the sense of a set of works of assured and unalterable value, distinguished by certain shared inherent properties, does not exist.
>
> (Eagleton, 1983: 10)

All this did have an impact on the thinking of a number of the young English graduates who left university and turned their faces towards secondary English teaching in the mid-1980s. What they brought with them, at first in that spirit of iconoclasm, and then as a more calmly internalized set of assumptions about English (for instance, feminist literary criticism and black women's writing, has become almost part of the mainstream of English studies), did contribute to a reconstitution of sorts in the subject paradigm, and in the recipes which expressed that.

Even within the academic field (leaving out the broad social and specific institutional changes mentioned earlier), it was not just a matter of one generation's idea of literary study attempting to supplant that of the previous generation, although that was part of the process. Notions of what was worth studying and taking seriously began to expand, to include the popular media, and anything else which by some stretch of the imagination might be called a text. There was, in effect, another whole complex history of media and cultural study that was also reaching maturity and making English studies different in the process.

In higher education, those changes go back to the French cultural theorists of the 1950s and 1960s, the foundation text here being Roland Barthes' *Mythologies*. In these essays, Barthes took the dreams of the long-dead linguist Ferdinand de Saussure about a non-existent discipline called semiotics, and synthesized these with the insights of anthropologists, Marxists and literary critics in order to reveal the cultural significance infusing the everyday phenomena of late-1950s' Paris: the Citroen DS, the meaning of red meat and wrestling. In the UK, in fact, the impact of Barthes' ideas was most notable, at first upon the new discipline of media studies that was quietly developing at the level of primary and secondary school education throughout the 1970s and early 1980s.

Way back in the 1930s, F.R. Leavis had argued the case for taking the popular media seriously within education ('seriously', for Leavis, of course meant an entirely hostile stance), and by the early 1960s a cautious but more liberal process of opening up education to the cultural realities of working class children had begun. The Newsom Report, *Half Our Future* (in effect, intended to address the needs of working-class children in schooling) suggested in 1963 that:

> . . . we should wish to add a strong claim for the study of film and television in their own right, as powerful forces in our culture and significant sources of language and ideas.
>
> (HMSO, 1963: para. 474)

Murdock and Phelps' study of media teaching at the end of that decade demonstrated that such an opening-up was still progressing only slowly, and it was at least a decade before significant advances in the development of a coherent discipline called 'media studies' (as against the odd lesson on the evils of advertising, or the occasional laboured study of high-quality, preferably Russian, films) in schools. Again, one must point to a combination of factors, such as developmental work done in the field of film studies in the early 1970s, the introduction of the video recorder into schools, and the progressive attitudes and energies of a few highly committed individuals.

Similarly, in the area of language study, the *Language in Use* project, based on the work of M.A.K. Halliday and developed by Doughty, Pearce and Thornton in the late 1960s, offered a means of introducing a sociolinguistic perspective to secondary school English teaching, especially for those children who made up the bulk of the comprehensive school population. The chief emphasis in this, and other work developed for use in schools around the same time, entailed 'rejecting the notion of correctness' and replacing it 'by the concept of appropriateness' (Mathieson, 1975: 147–8). During the early 1980s, it was at least possible to come across odd instances of a different kind of English taking shape. The Inner London Education Authority was a prime example of such a process, where a generous amount of funding, and shared political attitudes about the role of education in relation to race, gender, culture and class, had a direct impact on the work going on in a number of schools.

But these were isolated pockets of actual change, and the potential for more widespread change which they signalled remained unfulfilled throughout the early 1980s, despite the increasingly high public profile of organizations such as the ILEA English Centre, the British Film Institute's education department, or the National Association for the Teaching of English's increasing number of forays into literary theory, linguistics and media studies. The most insistent calls for change were in fact coming from higher education throughout this period, and that source did at least provide an increasing number of young graduates whose radically different views of English really seemed to suggest the prospect of imminent major change to English teaching throughout the secondary system. It seemed that the kind of breaking point that Raymond Williams spoke of – the moment of crisis in which a new paradigm comes into place – was about to occur.

Liberal humanists versus cultural theorists

The year 1986 was probably the peak of this process of change and still two clear, innocent years before the National Curriculum began to close down the horizons. Certainly to myself, engaged in the preparation of secondary English teachers, this seemed like an important and fruitful moment for investigating the kinds of subject paradigm that secondary English teachers were currently working within, and currently believed in. Working mainly with recent graduates of English, I was particularly interested in finding out the extent of mismatch between the subject paradigm which *some* recent graduates (given the radical nature of their views, often the most vocal) were bringing with them to their training, and that of the experienced teachers who would be supporting their learning in schools.

For this purpose, a questionnaire was devised which incorporated a range of beliefs and attitudes about different issues relevant to the teaching of English in secondary schools at that time. These attitudes and beliefs were taken (and adapted) from the kinds of sources already quoted in this chapter – subject department Statements of Aims, the writings of leading figures in the field – and were organized systematically to ensure adequate coverage of the two broad positions which seemed to characterize the main lines of thought in English teaching at the time: the apparently mainstream 'liberal humanist', personal growth, literature-centred view of English, and a more radical cultural theorist approach. There were four further subdivisions within these two

Table 2.1   Mainstream/liberal humanist versus radical/cultural theorist approach

Mainstream/liberal humanist	*Radical/cultural theorist*
Literature at the centre of English studies	Questioning the concept of literature
English studies for personal growth	The political dimension of language and literature studies
English as a means of educating taste and discrimination	Valuing popular culture and media study in English
Literary standard English as the ideal form of the language ('correctness')	Acceptance of students' own non-standard language use ('appropriateness')

broad categories, reflecting what was seen as specific ways in which those two overall approaches related to different aspects of the subject (Table 2.1). The whole questionnaire is included in the Appendix of this book. For all its inadequacies, it was quite a successful means of representing and examining some of the key areas of debate about the subject as it was being carried out in the mid-1980s. Some of the attitudes about, and claims for, English which seemed urgent then, now seem uncontentious and normal, some seem ludicrously out of date, and others now seem more radical than they did at the time.

The results were analysed in two ways: first of all by means of factor analysis, which uses a computer to reveal patterns of response not visible to the naked eye, and also simply through counting straight response figures relating to individual questions. The first method produced results which very firmly supported the division of views about English broadly into either liberal humanist or cultural theorist groups: these findings did suggest that the English teachers in this sample of roughly a hundred teachers (from a very mainstream authority, neither notably progressive nor particularly traditionalist) either strongly advocated notions such as personal growth, essentially through the study of literature and the engagement with imaginative, expressive writing, or they strongly rejected these in favour of a far more political, sociological approach to English studies, which dealt with very different texts and topics. These seemed to provide a valid and illuminating way of talking about the subject, although also evident in these results was a very strong and unanticipated element of idiosyncrasy. That is, although these teachers' thinking did relate well to the proposed dimension, there were other ways in which their preferences and dislikes were as individualized and personal – as resistant to the kind of gross generalization attempted earlier in this very paragraph – as English teachers have always claimed to be in their statements of belief about the subject.

Equally interesting, and slightly more easy to demonstrate in this account, were the individualized responses, which make particular sense in light of a further factor revealed by the computer analysis, i.e. that these teachers tended to eschew strong or extreme positions, whether radical or traditional. When not extreme, they appeared very open-minded and *liberal* about a wide range of attitudes concerning the nature of English, but there was generally little enthusiasm for heavy statements about any aspect of the subject, modern or traditional.

The questionnaire was answered on a five-point scale, offering the response choices 'Strongly agree', 'Agree', 'No clear response', 'Disagree' and 'Strongly disagree'. In order to efficiently capture the spirit of the results, the following examples will simply give the percentage of responses that combined 'Strongly agree' and 'Agree', so that it is possible at least to get a picture of the extent to which this particular selection of students were willing to give their assent to certain positions. For instance, an impressive 90 per cent of the respondents approved of the statement that:

> As English teachers, our business is to enable pupils to develop their reading tastes.
>
> (Item 41)

This is neither surprising nor contentious, given this statement's use of the word 'develop' rather than, say, 'change'. Perhaps more surprising is that 90 per cent of respondents *also* expressed approval for the following sentiment, already seen here in the extracts from the Statements of Aims:

> As teachers of English, we aim to awaken the sensitivity of our pupils to human emotions.
>
> (Item 42)

It is clear, therefore, that the personal growth model of the subject held a great attraction for this group of teachers, although not so many (a mere 59 per cent) were prepared to go to the extreme of laying themselves down beneath the metaphorical feet of their students in order to bring that about:

> The effective English teacher should act as a human bridge between childhood and adulthood.
>
> (Item 45)

In general, the liberal and open-minded attitudes of these teachers shines through time after time: 81 per cent considered that it was indeed 'the responsibility of the school to create an atmosphere of acceptance of all the children in its care and this involves an acceptance of their language'; 87 per cent thought that 'Good teaching of English at any level should concern itself with educating the sensibility and the emotions' (item 3), and whilst 88 per cent believed that literature was the best route in that respect ('The study of literature gives pupils the vocabulary with which to articulate their own maturing experience'; item 9); 89 per cent also agreed that 'We must make a claim for the study of film and TV in their own right as powerful forces in our culture and significant sources of language and ideas' (item 31).

They did *not* go for the suggestion that 'Our task in English should be to analyse discourses from a political vantage-point' (item 4; 15 per cent), although they did find a different wording of a similar sentiment more palatable: 'The teaching of language is a social and political act' (item 18; 51 per cent). They were also strongly opposed to the extreme nature of Frank Whitehead's claim that 'There are no "good" advertisements, only "effective" ones. In this field, education must always be negative – education against' (item 49; 9 per cent). Nor were they particularly taken by Matthew Arnold's belief that 'Good poetry does tend to form the soul and character' (item 25; 17 per cent).

The abiding impression of the majority of respondents is, therefore, of fairly open-minded people, who are willing to incorporate a wide variety of subject matter and perspectives in their teaching, as long as it was balanced and reasonable. An admirable mix of common sense, and idealism – the sort of decent if slightly pious sentiment expressed in the following, strongly approved (90 per cent) statement:

> I feel strongly that a major aspect of my role as a teacher of English is to foster feelings of awareness, sympathy, tolerance and understanding.
>
> (Item 20)

And yet, if one looks more closely – preferably with *unsympathetic* eyes – some of the views which earn the approval (78 per cent) of this particular set of teachers go quite far beyond what one might normally call *sensible*:

> The responsibility of teachers is to the experience of children, their minds, emotions and spirits: it is a matter of knowing the right sort of magic to lead one child from a closed alley of experience to an open one.
>
> (Item 39)

This is, whichever way you swing it, a fairly ambitious aspiration, a rather extreme form of liberal humanism. It is certainly not the sort of thing that would first come to mind faced with a group of thirty 12-year-olds in an English classroom – it reveals little about what is actually desirable *and* possible for a normal teacher to achieve. Such a statement, instead of helping to formulate plans of action, merely reveals the kinds of words which resonate well in the hearts and minds of English teachers. Such words belong in the 'recipes' of English teaching insofar as they create a sense of group identity, a feeling of group purpose, amongst English teachers, but these are poor recipes if they lead nowhere in terms of action. The same is true of the following statement, which by any rational standards means strictly nothing, but which gained an astonishing 72 per cent approval:

> English, more than any other subject, can have an extremely humanising effect.
>
> (Item 34)

Apart from the unfortunate implication that the students on whom this effect is to be wrought are *sub*-human until they get some English lessons inside them, I suppose that such vacuous and pious pronouncements might do little harm, if used sparingly. Presumably they at least made English teachers feel good about themselves and their work. But it does seem that back in those heady pre-National Curriculum days an extraordinarily high proportion of what English teachers had to say about their work functioned at the philosophical end of the Statement of Aims dimension, rather than the action end. And if one is not forced into working out the practical implications of one's aims – which involves thinking about how they might be translated into desirable outcomes for all students – then there is every chance that the feel-good satisfactions of boasting about the 'humanizing' effect of one's work are not likely to lead to much actual good in the classroom.

That, as I stated, is looking at such ways of talking about the subject through unsympathetic eyes, which is a necessary thing to do every now and then, if one is to think one's way into the job, rather than just get sucked into saying, believing and doing the same things as everybody else, just because everybody else says them. Many of the more ludicrous excesses in what teachers had to say about their work in the early 1980s do firmly belong to the past and, even if some of those lines of thought are less important to teachers now than they were then, that particular combination of claims about the *uniqueness*, the *humanizing power*, and the *flexibility* of English has lost its dominating force under the very different pressures which the National Curriculum has brought to bear on the job of English teaching. The job of making sense of that process, and of the aims for the subject which it has put into play, will be carried out in Chapter 3, so it is perhaps appropriate that – in the spirit of so many of the claims about English which this chapter has questioned – we leave it to John Dixon to sound an appropriate warning about the dangers of trying to pin English teaching down:

English is a quicksilver among metals – mobile, living and elusive. Its conflicting emphases challenge us today to look for a new, coherent definition. Its complexity invites the partial and incomplete view, the dangerous simplification that restricts what goes on in the classroom.

(Dixon, 1967)

3 The development of National Curriculum English

Class war returns to Britain's schools

Marxist teachers aiming to wreck education plans

A startling dossier revealing how the Left is seeking to dominate State school English teaching has been handed to the *Mail on Sunday*.

It discloses that an innocently named teaching association has drawn up a highly political agenda to challenge how the Government plans to improve standards in our 26,000 schools. The dossier was compiled by educational experts troubled by the direction the 3,000-strong National Association for the Teaching of English has taken. It contains records of speeches at private meetings and quotes from the association's literature. Whitehall officials, who have also seen it, claim that it confirms how Left-wing teachers and professors have accelerated the appalling decline in standards of reading and writing.

The dossier shows how the association's campaign has been frighteningly successful. Only last week examiners deplored the standards of grammar, spelling, punctuation and vocabulary of A-level candidates – children who have spent 13 years in our State system. . . .

It is clear from the dossier that many members are violently opposed to the formal teaching of English grammar.

The dossier alleges some of the association's followers – named in the dossier – have won top jobs on Government committees charged with the task of improving school standards.

Last night Education Minister John Patten said he was alarmed by the dossier's contents and said: 'I hope all teachers will join with me in condemning moves to bring politics into the teaching of English – which is, after all, one of the essential basics.' Dr John Marks, a key Government adviser on education, says: 'The teaching of English has become the main ideological weapon for those who want to politicise education in a left-wing direction.'

(*Mail On Sunday*, January 31 1993)

The teaching of English has always been an ideological weapon, but not simply for the politicizing of education in a Left-wing direction. In charting the process of formalizing the subject so that it can take up its place at the core of the National Curriculum, it is impossible to ignore the political tensions and prejudices which constantly intervened in what should properly have been entirely educational debates. It was, of course, particularly important that these educational debates should have been conducted thoughtfully and patiently, given both the nature of the planned National Curriculum and the particular disjointed history of English, but that was not allowed to happen.

As far as the National Curriculum is concerned, its fundamental problem is that it appears to have been designed on the back of a napkin – ten subjects is all you need, three core subjects (English, science and maths), get on with it. No-one remembered to leave space for anything fancy, like cross-curricular learning, so everything that was necessary had to be learned within the isolated and often inappropriate context of a single subject. As far as literacy is concerned, this would have been fine fifty, maybe one hundred, years earlier, when English was simply the place on the curriculum where literacy was taught. Unfortunately, because of English's history in subsequent years, things have changed, and its role has become far more specialized: it can no longer deliver the wide range of literacy/language skills which young people so desperately need if they are to succeed in education and beyond.

So the story of National Curriculum English mainly concerns the way in which politics got in the way of sorting out an inherent illogicality in the subject – over time, that illogicality has effectively developed into a deep fault-line between two kinds of English: one which tried to provide the general skills of language use that students might need at various moments in their life (a subject misguidedly viewed as being for working-class children only); another which increasingly began to introduce young people to their national literature (in 1918, The English Association suggested the study of literature as necessary for 'the continuity of national ideals'), and subsequently to various modes of consciousness and expression related to that literature, and its attendant values.

The fault-line in English Studies

One can, of course, argue for there being all sorts of intimate relations between the teaching of literacy and literature: you cannot study literature without literacy, so it might be possible to see literacy as a crucial stage on the way to the greater goal of literature study; also, you can interpret literacy very broadly (Paulo Freire, for instance, talks of reading the word and reading the *world*) and say that literacy encompasses and contains literature, among very many other forms of communication and ways of making meaning; you could even say that literature is itself a crucial stage on the way to the greater goal of full literacy. But the fact of a relationship is not in itself enough, because equally intimate relationships in fact exist between literacy and any number of other areas of human activity and study, and arguments that claim a special relationship between literacy and literature are simply rationalizing and sustaining the kind of English subject that has emerged over many, many years.

By the apparently more democratic 1960s, people like David Holbrook and John Dixon proposed and refined their notion of language and learning which appeared to accommodate and unite the two separate notions of literature and literacy, even if that did entail a certain degree of distortion to both. This accommodation taught us to see the main role for English teaching as being to help students use language in order to do things like build their 'own representational world' because 'In ordering and composing situations that in some way symbolise life as we know it, we bring order and composure to our inner selves' (Dixon, 1967; quoted in Chapter 2, p. 20). The general idea was that one could take the essence of literature – imaginative and symbolic explorations of individual human experience and human relationships – and marry that up with a sort of subject-specific notion of literacy, in which students' language resources developed through the explorations of their individual human experience and relationships. The great thing about this, as Dixon showed, was that you need not be restricted to the Great Tradition for your 'literature' – you could create a sort of lower-level canon which was still symbolic and inner, but was also usefully closer to children's interests and experience (for example, in the book *Kes*, in which a lonely boy struggles for personal growth out of the oppressions of working-class life, notably assisted by an English teacher). The key notion here was that English was *organic* (no question of any fault-line): you could not separate this democratic, non-nationalistic, personal growth notion of literature from its corresponding democratic, demotic, personal growth notion of literacy. English was all one, and must all be done as one, by one lot of people, in one classroom, under one banner: English. So deeply certain had this conviction become that it was very hard to detect any disagreement about this from within the ranks of the English teaching profession, even if a certain amount of kindly discrimination might have actually occurred in terms of what one might fairly expect from different kinds of children.

But those accommodations were not inspired by a reasoned and comprehensive conception of literacy, if you interpret the word to mean, simply, *the reading and writing skills that you need in life*. One can add *all* sorts of things to that (even, perhaps, oracy), but it would be difficult to argue that literacy could be anything *less* than that.

The 'reading and writing skills that you need in life' primarily involve, if you happen to be a student in school, all the multifold literacy skills which being a school student demands. As well as being able to cope with the emotional turmoil of growing up, young people also happen to need literacy in order to cope with the demands of studying different subjects. They require powerful skills of recording, organizing, analysing, reporting and reflecting critically upon the various things that need to be learnt. As they get older, further literacy demands can be identified, of course, such as those which people encounter as citizens, or as workers. And then there are the literacy skills needed to gain access to the pleasures and insights of aesthetic/imaginative writing, and to exercise the processes of such writing for oneself.

Obviously, the English subject area has become particularly good at teaching those last skills; that has always been a major aspect of its mission. It can also *contribute* to those other skills, to sharply varying degrees. Through its increasing engagements with media studies and sociolinguistics, it clearly has something to contribute to the literacy demands of citizenship. It can also dabble a bit in vocationally oriented literacy demands, in the minor opportunities it might provide for practice in job applications and interviews.

None of this is reason enough to assume, though, that the English subject area has ever been prepared or able to deal satisfactorily with that full range of reading and writing (and oral) skills to which all students are crucially entitled. English does an important job, but it is unreasonable to expect it to deliver full and general literacy. The failure of all attempts at devising a National Curriculum for English – the fault-line into which a million curriculum documents have so far been worthlessly stuffed – derives very significantly from the failure to think honestly about what can and cannot be achieved within any one slice of the curriculum, whatever name you give it.

The following sections work through the various attempts to arrive at a National Curriculum for the subject area called English that have been made since 1984. Undermining each attempt – however imaginative and radical – has been the same failure to be clear about what English can and cannot do. These difficulties have been compounded by the often ill-informed interventions of groups from outside the profession with privileged access to the media, although of course these same groups (whether speaking through the *Daily Mail* or *Daily Express*, through the Centre for Policy Studies, or through politicians) would insist that it was the professionals and not they who appropriated the National Curriculum.

As far as the development of the English curriculum is concerned, professional educators have often proved an equal match for those Right-wing forces who have tried to impose a simple and basic curriculum, but the point here is that this ideological conflict has consistently had the effect of exacerbating rather than resolving the fault-line that is hidden below the surface of the subject's rationale. The following sections will try to unfold both the development of what the professional educators came up with, and the corresponding attempts to reduce it to something more simple (or simple-minded, depending on your point of view).

English from 5 to 16 *(1984)*

English from 5 to 16, produced by Her Majesty's Inspectorate, marks the first tentative shot in the direction of a National Curriculum for English. In his introductory statement, Sir Keith Joseph offered an endorsement of the document's contents and explained that:

> We intend . . . in consultation with those concerned within and outside the education service, to move towards a statement of aims and objectives for English teaching in schools which can serve as a basis for policy at national and local level.
>
> (HMI, 1984)

This document, which was not particularly popular or admired, nonetheless provided the template for all subsequent attempts at a National Curriculum for English. In doing so, it has proved to be far more influential than the rather more impressive 'Bullock Report' (*A Language for Life*, DES, 1975) which directly preceded it. Whereas the Bullock Report was concerned with 'all aspects of teaching the use of English, including reading, writing, and speech' this document was about 'the aims of English teaching'. These might, at first sight, seem to be the same things (clearly they seemed so to the politicians who commissioned this and subsequent documents) but they are not: 'teaching the use of English' carefully refers to general literacy skills, whereas 'the aims of English teaching' refers only to the English subject area.

(Part of the problem of distinguishing between the two relates to the distinction between primary and secondary education. Obviously the situation is different at the primary level, where one might reasonably argue English only exists on a cross-curricular basis. But the influence of the structures of secondary education dominates – as the design of the National Curriculum incontrovertibly demonstrates – and even in primary school literacy teaching increasingly becomes grounded in the typical content of the English subject area. In this book, the focus is on the secondary version of the subject, but the problems created in that focus do exist lower down the age range.)

The Bullock Committee understood these issues well, and explored broad questions of literacy, especially in relation to learning, in terms of the *whole curriculum*, rather than just that part of the curriculum taught in English lessons by English teachers. Given that fact, it was perfectly reasonable and appropriate that the Bullock Report should have adopted as an organizing device the broad categories of reading, writing and speech (although it did not restrict itself to those categories). Unfortunately, though, *English from 5 to 16* was exclusively concerned with the English subject area, and was very little concerned with a cross-curricular perspective – it was therefore completely inappropriate that it should select as its main organizing structure for English the same broad and general categories as Bullock.

English from 5 to 16 referred to these as the 'four modes of language':

- listening
- speaking
- reading
- writing

Whilst these four 'modes' ('speaking' and 'listening' were placed together in actual fact) might have a certain validity in terms of general literacy, as clinically measurable skills which develop differentially, they are simply not valid as distinct elements of the English curriculum, to be taught and assessed in isolation from each other. Yet, as a result of this misreading of the Bullock Report, we have been stuck ever since with a means of organizing the English curriculum which bears very little direct relation to the way things are taught and learnt in English classrooms. It was a disastrous decision.

This document had one other equally long-term (although by no means disastrous) impact upon the English curriculum in its attempt to create a separate add-on concept to the English curriculum that *eventually* became known as knowledge about language. This was not an established term in the 1984 document, being introduced here as 'a fourth aim which applies over all the modes of language. This is to teach children *about* language . . .' (The document goes on to offer this explanation: 'so that they achieve a working knowledge of its structure and of the variety of ways in which meaning is made, so that they have a vocabulary for discussing it, so that they can use it with greater awareness, and because it is interesting.')

There was, and continued to be, a certain desperation in the rationale for this approach to developing literacy. The politicians were telling the professionals to tell children how to write properly, and the professionals tried to think of a way of doing so that reflected their own theories of how understanding develops. In a way it was a good compromise, and certainly led to some fascinating developments within the subject that were entirely appropriate to a subject ostensibly concerned with the English language, but it also fostered the illusion – especially in the way it was linked to those 'four modes of language' – that English now had the whole problem of general literacy wrapped up.

From the very start, though, *English from 5 to 16* fudged the distinction between specialist English and general literacy:

> Achieving competence in the many and varied uses of our language is a vital part of the education of pupils in our schools. All teachers, whatever their other responsibilities and whatever age groups they teach, have a contribution to make to this process . . . However, in every school there are teachers who have direct responsibility for the development of their pupils' competence in English.
>
> (HMI, 1984, paras 1.1 and 1.2)

The fudge is in the use of the word 'English' here: that elision of subject name and language name simply deepens the fault-line in English that ultimately renders hopeless all attempts at coherence in the subject's structure.

Laying the ground for National Curriculum English – Kingman and the Centre for Policy Studies

The elision of English-the-subject with English-the-language reached epic proportions in the next stage of the journey, the report of the Kingman Committee's

Inquiry into the Teaching of English Language, set up in early 1987 by Kenneth Baker. If you detect a slight note of ambiguity in the report's title (is this about a cross-curricular language policy, or is it about English teaching?) do not expect to achieve clarification in its terms of reference, which stated that the report was 'to recommend a model of the English language as a basis for teacher training and professional discussion, and to consider how far and in what ways that model should be made explicit at various stages of education'.

The report's designated job was to take the speculations of *English from 5 to 16* about teaching and learning about language, and give those substance. The English teaching profession (which thought that the report would contain a first draft of National Curriculum English) feared that this would be a Right-wing attempt at the reintroduction of prescriptive grammar, but in the event the report merely offered English teachers some fairly academic kinds of linguistic knowledge which might be incorporated into their subject teaching. These suggestions do provide a good starting point for new English subject content – study about the English language – but the considerable detail of this report actually goes no further than the previous document in justifying the hypothesis that knowledge about language leads directly to increased literacy. Its attempt to argue that knowledge *about* language structures leads to mastery *of* those structures is, in fact, famously limp:

> It is arguable that such mastery might be achieved without explicit knowledge of the structure of the language or the ways it is used in society. But there is no positive advantage in such ignorance.
>
> (DES, 1988: para. 12)

The point is not whether such knowledge sets back the development of literacy (which in fact it certainly *could* do, if it was done badly enough to muddle learners, or waste their precious time), but whether it actually advances it. Clearly it is appropriate for English teachers to explore the possibilities of new subject content such as this, but that is not actually what is promised in the report's title. In the event, the Kingman Report actually succeeded in justifying Right-wing fears about professionals making everything too complex and too clever by half – it delivered precious few firm statements about what is correct and incorrect in English language usage, which teachers could be made to teach.

Fearful of just such an outcome, in fact, the Right had tried to get its retaliation in first, having fired a warning shot at the Kingman Committee in the shape of a 44-page pamphlet published by the Right-wing Centre for Policy Studies (CPS) in 1987: the remarkable *English our English*, by one John Marenbon (a Cambridge University medievalist, coincidentally the husband of Sheila Lawlor, then Deputy Director of the Centre for Policy Studies). The one paragraph Introduction sets the mood with startling clarity, and some rather unscholarly exaggeration:

When children leave English schools today, few are able to speak and write English correctly; even fewer have a familiarity with the literary heritage of the language. It is not hard to see why. Among those who theorise about English teaching there has developed a new orthodoxy, which regards it as a conceptual error to speak of 'correct' English and which rejects the idea of a literary heritage. The new orthodoxy has now come to influence every aspect of English in schools – from curricula to teaching in the classroom to public examinations. Her Majesty's Inspectorate is among its staunch proponents. The object of this pamphlet is to describe the new orthodoxy; to examine how its views have spread; and to consider whether its tenets are convincing, and whether English might be taught better.

(Marenbon, 1987: 5)

The Kingman Report took not a blind bit of notice of this document, of course, but neither did it achieve a great deal in its own right, such as getting anyone to take seriously its important recommendation that prospective teachers of English/literacy should study linguistic knowledge and language development as part of their first degrees. But it did pick up the half-baked hot potato of teaching knowledge about language in the secondary school which the 1984 *English from 5 to 16* had put into play, and pass it on to the Cox Committee, whose job of writing the real National Curriculum English was announced on the day the Kingman Report was published.

National Curriculum English: the CPS overture

When Kenneth Baker announced proposals for a National Curriculum in 1987, he totally ignored the advice of organizations such as HMI, which had tried in 1985 to develop a framework for a modern curriculum by outlining 'areas of learning and experience' and 'elements of learning' that were not subject specific (DES, 1985: 16). Despite the pleas from Eric Bolton, then Chief Inspector, that the curriculum should be designed by people 'who know what they are talking about' as against politicians and administrators (quoted in Chitty, 1989: 123), Baker blundered on and created a curriculum consisting of ten traditional and unrelated subjects (for which there was not even adequate space on the school timetable).

For at least twenty years before the National Curriculum, a small number of Right-wing Tories with a particular interest in education tried to establish a firm and sensible direction for Tory educational policy (see Christopher Knight's detailed account in *The Making of Tory Education Policy in Post-War Britain 1950–1986*, and Clyde Chitty's slightly more balanced *Towards a New Education System: the Victory of the New Right?*) based on the idea that the only good curriculum was a simple one. At the heart of these efforts was a conviction about the need for a National Curriculum which would both maintain basic standards and help establish a market-driven, rather than teacher-driven, school system. The fundamental idea was that so long as schools could ensure that students knew the basic curriculum, individual schools could teach whatever they liked, and parents would make that succeed or fail by their marketplace choices. Such thinking depends, of course, on the highly questionable but absolutely essential element of Right-wing educational belief which says that *basic* educational ideals are obvious – mere common sense. The 1975 article by Rhodes Boyson ('Maps, Chaps and Your Hundred Best Books') that Peter Benton refers to in Chapter 5 of this book is a prime example of that belief.

The Centre for Policy Studies became the prime mouthpiece for this view of education. This time, Sheila Lawlor herself wrote a little pamphlet, called *Correct Core: Simple Curricula for English, Maths and Science* (note the 'Correct', note the 'Simple'). What she has to say about English is entirely in the same spirit as Marenbon discussed above, although she does get to the point in a slightly more brisk manner. In terms of English, at any rate, what she comes up with turns out to be neither illuminating or simple. For a start, like most who came before and after her, she does not make sense of the relationship between 'basic literacy' and whatever it is that goes on in the English subject area, claiming that the National Curriculum 'should not set out a complete teaching scheme, but indicate the minimum fundamental levels of knowledge and skills without which there can be no further progress in the wider subject'. Her vision of English is prehistoric, a muddled recollection of some kind of relationship between great literature and basic literacy, and her suggestions are stodgy and lifeless.

Lawlor therefore misses a great opportunity, because a convincing vision of simplicity could have been immensely useful just at that moment when the Cox Committee members were sharpening their pencils and hunkering down for some seriously complex curriculum writing.

The Cox Reports and the first version of National Curriculum English

There is a great deal to be said in favour of the two reports of the Cox Committee, but most of it has already been said in considerable detail by Brian Cox himself, in the memorably titled *Cox on Cox*. There is no need to reiterate that story here, including the process of development from the first report *English for ages 5 to 11* to the second report *English for ages 5 to 16*, and instead I intend merely to pick out the trends in the design of the English curriculum which it notably carried on or introduced.

For the purposes of this summative account, the important point to emphasize is that the key structural characteristics of this report were already visible in the 1984 *English from 5–16*. The Cox committee maintains that report's division of the English subject area into the four (or is it three?) 'modes' of speaking & listening, reading and writing. It also very seriously takes forward that report's idea about focusing additionally on teaching and learning about language, picking up where the Kingman Committee (of which Cox had been a member) left off by trying to turn its fundamentally academic ideas into something nearer a programme for teaching.

These attempts were considerably more important than what has become the most quoted aspect of the Cox Committee's two reports: the attempt to acknowledge and create some consensus between different ideologies of English teaching, in the hope that such differences might be reconciled through informed debate.

> It is possible to identify within the English teaching profession a number of different views of the subject. We list them here, though we stress that they are not the only possible views, they are not sharply distinguishable, and they are certainly not mutually exclusive.
>
> (DES, 1989: para. 2.20)

The report goes on to summarize five views of English teaching, which it identifies as *personal growth, cross-curricular, adult needs, cultural heritage* and *cultural analysis*. These categories have been useful in demonstrating the increasingly plural nature of attitudes to English teaching, but the quality of analysis is shaky: 'cultural heritage', 'personal growth' and 'adult needs' are simply different aspects of one view of English, all of which implicitly or explicitly take for granted the privileged status of English literature, but in ways that vary according to a long-established perception of the differing needs of students from different social classes. To a large extent, therefore, these do not really represent different views at all, whereas a 'cultural analysis' viewpoint is so firmly opposed to beliefs about the inherent superiority of particular forms of language and literature that it could never be reconciled with the previous three. In addition, it is meaningless to talk of a 'cross-curricular' view of the English subject area, or of any particular subject. The whole point – which the Bullock Report understood quite clearly in trying to establish a cross-curricular view of learning to use the English language – is that the relationship between the English subject area and the rest of literacy learning needed to be examined and developed. Needless to say, given its misconception about this issue, the Cox Committee did not manage that.

These five views are mainly interesting in that they demonstrate the general determination of the Cox Committee to take current changes and developments in the subject into account. Ideologically, it looked like all the simplistically traditionalistic arguments from CPS and the *Daily Mail* and *Daily Express* had not won the day after all. For instance, both versions of the Cox Report quote the Kingman Report's strongly democratic rationale for expertise in language:

> People need expertise in language to be able to participate effectively in a democracy. There is no point in having access to information that you cannot understand . . . A democratic society needs people who have the linguistic abilities which will enable them to discuss, evaluate and make sense of what they are told, as well as to take effective action on the basis of their understanding . . . Otherwise

there can be no genuine participation, but only the imposition of the ideas of those who are linguistically capable.

(DES, 1989, para. 17.20)

Such talk of empowerment is verging on the revolutionary, and is by no means inconsistent with Michael Apple's overtly Marxist analysis of education in *Ideology and the Curriculum*:

> One way to think about culture in society is to employ a metaphor of distribution. That is, one can think about knowledge as being unevenly distributed among social and economic classes, occupational groups, different age groups, and groups of different power. Thus, some groups have access to knowledge distributed to them and not distributed to others. The obverse of this is also probably true. The *lack* of certain kinds of knowledge – where your particular group stands in the complex process of cultural preservation and distribution – is related, no doubt, to the absence in that group of certain kinds of political and economic power in society.
>
> (Apple, 1979: 17)

In general, the Cox proposals succeed in advancing the quality and breadth of discourse about English, and clearly have none of the repressive spirit which English teachers had feared, given that the head of the committee had originally been appointed on the strength of his deep involvement with the educational Right during the 1960s and early 1970s. The report therefore came as a considerable relief to English teachers, *in general*.

In its particulars, though, it was perhaps felt to be rather less satisfactory. A good number of English teachers were worried that they would have to start teaching topics and content about which they knew little: media studies, and knowledge about language, for instance (although some others were disappointed that there was not greater insistence on these things). More fundamental were the problems posed by the overall organization of the material which amounted to a set of checklists rather than a clearly structured curriculum through which one might chart a clear and logical course.

Two fundamental problems come to mind first of all, which proved to be a major weakness of the statutory version of the Cox curriculum which was published in March 1990, after an additional period of revision, argument and further revision:

1 The division of the English curriculum into the three or four modes of language, creates some strange anomalies, exacerbated by the attempt to integrate the knowledge about language requirements.
2 The document presents the assessment criteria – the Statements of Attainment – first, and relegates the Programmes of Study, which specify the actual teaching to be undertaken, to the back of the document, where they tended to be ignored (neither did it help that the items in the Programmes of Study, unlike the Statements of Attainment, were not adequately numbered, making discussion or analysis of them slow and laborious).

The design fault of dividing English into speaking, listening, reading and writing becomes truly evident in the final version of the 1990 curriculum orders. Consider, for example, the following Statements of Attainment, and try to guess which one belongs in the Speaking & Listening Attainment Target, which in the Reading, and which in the Writing:

1 Demonstrate in discussion and writing knowledge of ways in which language varies between different types of texts.
2 Demonstrate knowledge of oganisational differences between spoken and written English.
3 Demonstrate, in talking and writing about a range of stories and poems which they have read, an ability to explain preferences.
4 Demonstrate in discussion and in writing some understanding of attitudes in society towards language change and of ideas about appropriateness and correctness in language use.

or the following from the Programmes of Study:

5 Literary texts (including drama scripts), the use of language, responses to the media, pupils' own written work and the use of information technology might furnish many of the materials and topics for discussion for which planned outcomes, e.g. in written work or presentations, might emerge.
(Detailed provision for Key Stages 3 and 4: para. 18)

The answers are, in fact, as follows:

1 Writing (Statement of Attainment 9d).
2 Writing (Statement of Attainment 8d).
3 Reading (Statement of Attainment 5a).
4 Reading (Statement of Attainment 10e).
5 Speaking and listening (from the detailed provision for Key Stages 3 and 4).

It is fairly difficult to locate a consistent logic behind these choices. Not only is it obviously impossible to develop or assess any of these discrete language 'modes' without recourse to one or both of the others, but also some of these terms of assessment have nothing whatsoever to do with *any* of the modes: for instance, 'an ability to explain preferences' is clearly something in addition to, and different from, a 'mode of language'.

Some of these confusions can fairly be attributed to the novelty of the task of writing an all-embracing National Curriculum. Despite what the Right-wing say about how such a curriculum should be, the moment anyone tries to produce one, basic requirements of clarity, precision and sufficient coverage of all necessary bases means that things get complex, however hard one tries to avoid that. Even Sheila Lawlor's attempt at a simple curriculum is horribly full of complexity and anomalies. Above all, though, the problems signalled by the above extracts from the Curriculum result from the wholly unsatisfactory structure which was now well in place and clearly hard to break out of. But it is a pity – especially given the immense qualities of fresh thinking and imagination that went into the Cox Curriculum – that it allowed itself to be stuck with that structure, because as a result, English continues to be stuck with it.

From Cox to cock-up: the interim period

Teachers set about implementing the sometimes bewildering range of demands contained in the first version of the National Curriculum in September 1990. A certain amount of media study began to happen in every school, and Shakespeare (the only writer specified in the Cox Curriculum) came rapidly back into fashion, mainly with an emphasis on accessibility and the dramatic pleasures that his plays had to offer rather than on the basis of a more traditional textual analysis. There were serious attempts, too, to stretch the kinds of text and uses of language studied beyond the realms of imaginative literature to incorporate persuasive language and information gathering (moves initiated a few years earlier in the later years of the secondary school by GCSE). The absolute dominance of the class reader as the main structural determinant of what went on in English began to recede – slightly.

Of particular significance, it seemed, was the way English teachers began to take on the teaching of knowledge about language. Students started to learn about things like the history of the language, and about the differences between dialect and standard English, and about how those things related to notions such as accent and Received Pronunciation. The ultimate idea – and the thing that justifies the original inclusion of this approach in the 1984 HMI document – was that students would be taught how to articulate and explore their own understandings about language, and skills at using it. In order to advance these processes, a considerable amount of government money was devoted to an exciting and visionary project called LINC (Language in the National Curriculum), which was to produce materials for training teachers in knowledge about language, and in ways of teaching that.

English teachers who had, until very recently, set a premium on flexibility and the freedom to do one's own thing, now increasingly got together in their departments and collaborated on the production of coherent plans of work and teaching materials, as the following comment from a member of a comprehensive English Department testifies: 'If the National Curriculum has done anything, it's made us really think about our aims, our objectives and what we are trying to do' (in Cooper and Davies, 1993). There was a general recognition of the need to expand subject knowledge and content, and to be organized in doing so and, despite the strong reservations that the English teaching profession had about it in advance, there was a strong and positive feeling that the National Curriculum had reinvigorated the teaching of English, and had had a positive influence not merely on content, but on ways of teaching:

> it would be impossible to fulfil the National Curriculum and just stand at the front of the class. . . . You've only got to look at what's on offer in the English

curriculum to see that there is a notion of what is good practice behind [it]; behind that: what is good teaching and learning.

(Davies, 1993)

Even at a more basic level, English teachers were recognising that the National Curriculum provided a route out of the inevitable inertia that settles after a number of years doing the same thing, and solving the same problems:

> I quite like it because it's a checklist for me, because I know I can slip into what's easy for me. . . . And it makes me try – has made me try different things. And I think that's a good thing.

(Cooper and McIntyre, 1996: 53)

Of course, there is always a tendency to rewrite the past as things get steadily worse but it does seem that, after two years in operation, the majority of English teachers were energetic and optimistic in their response to the demands of National Curriculum English. According to the newsletter of the National Association for the Teaching of English:

> Many members will be aware of the evidence collected by NATE's research officer, John Johnson, and by the National Association of Advisers of English, demonstrating the success of schools in implementing the National Curriculum, and arguing for no change.

(Editorial, *NATE News*, Autumn 1992)

So why on earth would anyone be talking about changing the Curriculum so soon after it had first been implemented?

Rewriting the English Orders

In July 1992, *not two years* after English teachers started to teach National Curriculum English, the Government published a document called *National Curriculum English: The Case for Revising the Order*, which began with the following reassurance:

> We recognise that our proposals are likely to be controversial. We have given careful consideration to the argument that any decision to revise what is a popular order will undermine morale and prejudice the progress which has been made since the introduction of National Curriculum English. This would certainly be a valid point if we were proposing to overturn the underlying rationale and achievements of the current Order. We intend, however, to develop the strengths of the current Order . . .

(NCC, July 1992)

This is dishonest. The aim clearly was to destroy the Cox Curriculum as comprehensively as possible, partly just out of revenge for the way Cox himself had turned native and fallen for all that rubbish about teaching appropriate rather than correct ways of using language, and about different views of English. The greatest crime was in failing to come up with the few good clear rules for correct English that had been expected of him. Given that the professionals in the National Curriculum Council understood that the views of the extreme right had to be satisfied, but that their formulations were simply unworkable, every effort was made to phrase this insistence on simple rules for correctness with some academic respectability: thus the term 'standard English' (something halfway between the linguistic concept 'Standard English', and a more common sense notion of 'normal' English) was now awarded a more senior role in the subject's conceptual hierarchy:

> The one explicit reference to standard English in the statements of attainment [in the Cox curriculum] focuses on the need to develop 'an awareness of grammatical differences between spoken standard English and a non-standard variety' (level 6). This is not the same thing as being able to use standard English in conversation and will not necessarily encourage pupils to speak clearly, accurately and confidently. . . . These requirements need to be based on a clear definition of standard English.
>
> (NCC, 1992: para. 11)

These views were back up in the press at the time by David Pascall, then Chairman of NCC, who demanded all children should be taught to speak properly, even in the playground. In such a climate (only the previous year, Kenneth Clarke had suddenly and brutally abandoned the LINC project, which had also failed to come up with a few simple rules for correct English) the decision to revise the whole English curriculum felt like just one more twist in the process of winding back the clock.

Key Stage 3 English tests

This process of destruction and revision was not made any more bearable by the unfortunate business of the Key Stage 3 English testing which John Patten, the Secretary of State tried to impose later in 1992. The proposed testing, quite remarkably, bore no relation to the teaching and attainments specified in the National Curriculum (which, of course, the teachers had been faithfully working towards since 1990). It was this process which brought Dr Marenbon back into the public eye at this as – somewhat mysteriously – Chairman of English committee of the Schools Examination and Assessment Council.

As it turned out (much to the warm appreciation of the profession) Marenbon had a bad time of the experience, and joined a number of the other deserters from Patten's ship. Marenbon clearly did not feel comfortable at having to argue for any universal kind of English teaching. He decided that 'students of less than average ability [should] concentrate on mastering the basics [and government should] give up the fruitless attempt to set out a standard approach to literature for all teachers and all students' (*The Times*, May 10 1993). In this argument, we appear to return to the nineteenth century idea of two completely different English curriculums: one in which bright (that is, middle class) children are inducted into a national culture, and another in which working–class children became at least sufficiently literate. As Marenbon confesses 'Traditionalists like myself might be tempted to feel regret at giving up the chance to ensure that all children are introduced to some of the great literary classics [but what the hey!] the love of literature is not something which can be instilled by order'.

Marenbon was right at least in his conclusion that these tests were bad news. There were a number of reasons for this: they were administered in such a way that they forced the rapid reintroduction of ability setting, right in the middle of the year; they forced the abandonment of a planned curriculum; they introduced out-moded forms of study, such as anthologies of literary extracts; and they turned the study of Shakespeare from one element within the English curriculum to the very epicentre of all English activities. The insensitive and bullying manner of their introduction left teachers with no choice but to protest, and to risk trouble from Heads and Governors, when this was the last thing most of them actually wanted. They were left feeling powerless and worthless, as the following comments (collected by myself at the time in an attempt to monitor what were clearly extraordinary events), demonstrate:

'. . . when this [changes at Key Stage 4] is taken along with the Key Stage 3 business, a lot of experienced teachers have not coped – they've come to me and said they are not coping and why should they be made to feel like that – they are professional people who like to plan ahead.'

(Head of English, School A)

'. . . these people [members of English department] are being massively deskilled'.

(Head of English, School T)

'We all of us felt that our professionalism had been undermined because we were not able say to children this is the course that we're teaching, this is what I want from you because it was changing.'

(Head of English, School J)

'I think a lot of people, especially experienced teachers who know what they're doing, have found it insulting, and have found it demoralizing. Er, I think it's sad when I see colleagues, even new staff, you know, desperately scrabbling to see what the tests contain and to see what the set texts are, because I know that a lot of people will abandon their experience and start to just teach to the tests.'

(Head of English, School Q)

'Personally, I feel angry rather than of low morale, finding anger an energizing agent. Hopefully, I will through this anger develop Lear's self-knowledge rather than his madness and self-destruction. Control – slipping! Part of me wishes that "they" would take all our decisions for us, not just what to teach, but when and how to teach it.'

(Head of English, School L)

It was certainly not the case that all the teachers were unambiguously opposed to the idea of testing, or to the subject content which the tests effectively imposed upon the existing curriculum:

> 'I'm quite pleased myself that people have tackled the Shakespeare, cause I think, they've found it more fun than they would've thought, and the kids have enjoyed it, on the whole. Er, so, in a way it, it, it's an unexpected thing that's, a bonus that's come out of it.'
>
> (Head of English, School Q)

> 'Quite a few teachers took two or three things out of the anthology basically because they actually liked some of the things that were there.'
>
> (Head of English, School Y)

These last remarks signal what turned out to be a crucial development. The English teachers were clearly furious at the way everything to which they had committed themselves over previous years – GCSE, the National Curriculum – was being unpicked before their eyes, and the imposition of these tests quite evidently turned out to be the last straw. For an interesting combination of reasons – Patten's own incompetence, the good timing of union interventions, the unexpected support of parents, the heroic stand made by certain Heads at certain moments, etc. – the teachers found themselves boycotting the tests. But this did not mean that all of them actually wanted to go that far, or that all of them were truly opposed to the more traditional version of the subject the tests had helped to reinstate. One might even go so far as to say that a combination of familiarity with the more traditional forms of content and teaching method felt quite welcome, after such a prolonged period of innovation, change and uncertainty.

In effect, this is the moment when the Right-wing did actually win its battle to take control of English teaching, even if the defeat of Patten, various resignations, and emollient noises from Sir Ron Dearing made it seem otherwise. The battle over these tests was when the English curriculum really changed, when all the decent ideas in the Cox Curriculum – at any rate, the openings it provided for working towards a more appropriate and forward-looking English curriculum – were turned over and buried again, and the past was triumphantly resurrected.

Although the discovery by many teachers that Shakespeare could be taught with some apparent success to students of all ages (if you spent enough time and effort doing so) hardly seems inappropriate to the English subject area, I wish to suggest that that, and indeed the whole emphasis on a highly structured, traditionalist, test-oriented curriculum, has actually sent English teaching in entirely the wrong direction. The effect has been to bring to an end, for the time being, all attempts at developing the subject so that it could eventually engage with the linguistic, cultural and technological demands of the late twentieth century. Those demands are about the struggle to make sense of the world that young people live in, as they try to establish their own place in that world, through language. English has a very special role to play here, but there is currently very little prospect of that happening if there is only time for *Romeo and Juliet*.

The end of the road: the revised National Curriculum

In December 1993, Sir Ron Dearing published a report on how to simplify the whole of the National Curriculum. The aim was to:

> reduce the volume of material required by law to be taught; simplify and clarify the programmes of study; reduce prescription so as to give more scope for professional judgement; ensure that the Orders are written in a way which offers maximum support to the classroom teacher.
>
> (HMSO, 1993: para. 3.8)

The way the popular version of the story goes is that the Government recognized that it had asked too much, that the profession had had enough, and this was a climb-down, turnaround and general concession to good sense.

So it is funny, really, that what we end up with is pretty much like what the Right-wing was asking for all along. Sheila Lawlor began her advice on writing a National Curriculum by asserting that the National Curriculum should not 'attempt to do more than set minimum standards in basic knowledge and technique'. Of course, one could not expect the professionals to provide this, because 'the official committees, the DES and Her Majesty's Inspectorate no longer adhere to the belief that teachers should teach and pupils should learn a simple body of knowledge and a simple set of techniques'. The aims of the Curriculum should, she claimed, both 'raise standards for all pupils' and give 'greater responsibility to those most directly concerned with the education of the young' (Lawlor, 1988). Which is exactly what Dearing came up with, albeit in slightly sweeter terms.

It is not entirely clear, therefore, whether or not this is what the profession actually wanted, or what the Right-wing wanted it to want. It certainly remains to be seen whether the new English curriculum is what the English teachers want, but there are a few points worth making about what actually underlies what appears at first glimpse to be an uninspiring but inoffensive little document.

English in the National Curriculum in 1995

It seems that SCAA (the Schools Curriculum and Assessment Authority, which now runs both curriculum and assessment nationally) did a superb public relations job on this latest version of the English subject area, because the current professional consensus seems to view the new English curriculum quite fondly, claiming (a) it is not as bad as was feared, and (b) it leaves teachers free to do whatever they want once again. This is consistent with the view that, given the appalling pressures under which English teachers have had to work in recent years, it might be pleasant just to settle into a familiar version of the subject, and a comfortable freedom of manoeuvre. However, I think we need to argue against such a view, because it too easily allows any progress made on the long journey towards this current version of English to be lost for ever.

I will ignore the vast bulk of the document (which any concerned person simply must read for themselves, after all, given its legal status), and concentrate on just two important issues: (i) the fundamental rationale for English which this document continues to promote (once more eliding the subject with literacy in general); and (ii) the notion of standard English which supposedly underlies the document, and which was such a major part of the justification for rewriting it in the first place.

The underlying notion of English

> English should develop pupils' abilities to communicate effectively in speech and writing and to listen with understanding. It should also enable them to be enthusiastic, responsive and knowledgeable readers.
>
> > (DFE, 1995: para. 1, p. 2)

This opening paragraph is offered as a summative statement about the English curriculum, and therefore its unambiguous assertion that the subject 'English' is concerned with broad language development must be taken very seriously. Because the English Orders say nothing about the extent to which this responsibility for language development is shared with other subjects (the above statement *is* ambiguous in this respect), it is sensible first of all to investigate what the other new subject orders have to say about this.

There is indeed a reference of sorts to literacy and oracy in the Common Requirements which come at the start of the documents for all other subjects, apart from Modern Languages and PE:

> **Use of Language**
> Pupils should be taught to express themselves clearly in both speech and writing and to develop their reading skills. They should be taught to use grammatically correct sentences and to spell and punctuate accurately in order to communicate effectively in written English.

This really does not help a great deal. It says nothing about enabling children to develop skills of reading, writing and oracy in order to get access to, organize, analyse and report their learning in any of these subjects; it just says that teachers of all subjects must contribute to general standards of linguistic correctness, especially in their writing. (It says literally nothing about helping children to read.) Specific subject documents deal intermittently with subject specific aspects of literacy, but mainly only in relation to learning the language of the subject (for example 'organise their knowledge and understanding of history through the accurate selection and deployment of terms necessary to describe and explain the periods and topics studied'; 'Pupils should be taught to use an extended geographical vocabulary'). On some occasions, there are actually mentions of the literacy skills pupils need to attain for success in the subject ('Pupils should be taught to communicate their knowledge and understanding of history, using a range of techniques, including extended narratives and descriptions, and substantiated explanations') but nowhere in any of these curriculum documents is there any hint of guidance to teachers about the need to systematically develop such skills. This must count as a serious omission, for which one might consider a range of explanations: either (a) the people that designed these curriculum documents do not believe that there *are* specific, teachable literacy skills which students need in order to learn successfully; or (b) they do think these skills exist, but it is not the business of the National Curriculum to specify them (perhaps they are perceived to operate at the level of classroom management); or (c) it is presumed that *this is what English teaching does*. If that is the case, then we have to take that opening paragraph of the English curriculum very seriously indeed, as a promise that the new English curriculum is about to undertake the development of the full range of literacy skills, on behalf of all the other subjects.

So, what are the specifications for the development of general literacy skills in the English curriculum? If they are not there, then they are not anywhere; which turns out to be precisely the case. The most vivid example in this respect is the specification for Reading at Key Stages 3 and 4 of the National Curriculum, in the only subject area of the whole National Curriculum which explicitly deals with reading. The first section addresses the question of the Range of reading to be ensured:

> (a) Pupils should be given opportunities to read a wide variety of literature, and to respond to the substance and style of texts. They should also be encouraged to read widely and independently solely for enjoyment. Some texts should be studied in detail, but the main emphasis should be on the encouragement of wider reading in order to develop independent, responsive, and enthusiastic readers . . .

All fairly legitimate stuff within the bounds of English as a specialist subject, with the same degree of specialist preoccupations as all other subjects, but there is very little more than this. Two highly detailed pages of specifications about literature follow. Section (b) specifies the kinds of literature to be studied – plays, novels and short stories, poetry and the work of individual poets. Section (c) makes *very* superficial mention of the multicultural dimension ('Pupils should read texts from other cultures and traditions that represent their distinctive voices and forms, and offer varied perspectives and subject matter'), whilst Section (d) details the names of actual literary authors to be studied (at great length). Section (f) mentions the media, cravenly placating political masters by insisting that any magazine, newspaper, radio, television or film texts that are studied 'should be of high quality', which rather misses the point of media studies (see Chapter 4).

Section (e) engages with all the other kinds of reading one might do in life (like being able to read about science, politics, the environment, economics, getting jobs, maths, computers, technology, sport, sociology, statistics, the world at large, and learn what you need from that reading) as follows:

> (e) Pupils should be introduced to a wide range of non-fiction texts, e.g. auto-biographies, biographies, journals, diaries, letters, travel writing, leaflets. They should be given opportunities to read texts that show quality in language use, and portray information, issues and events relating to contemporary life or past experience in ways that are interesting and challenging.

(DFE, 1995: 20)

Under Key Skills, the next category of reading specifications, there is an important requirement that:

> Pupils should be given opportunities to read factual and informative texts in order to:
> - Select information.
> - Compare and synthesise information drawn from different texts, e.g. IT-based sources and printed articles.
> - Make effective use of information in their own work.
> - Evaluate how information is presented.
> - In using information sources, pupils should be taught to sift the relevant from the irrelevant, and to distinguish between fact and opinion, bias and objectivity.

(DFE, 1995: 21)

This is hot air, simply covering up the fact the National Curriculum makes no realistic provision for learning of this kind. The English subject area itself does not, and indeed *should* not, try to give such opportunities to students, because those opportunities are what all students already possess in bewildering abundance, right across the curriculum. What they *lack* is knowledge of how to benefit from such opportunities, and nothing in this document even begins to address how to provide that knowledge. (The same story can be told about the provisions for Writing in this version of the English curriculum.) Given the facts that the English document begins by implying that it *does* deal with these, that the other curriculum documents do not engage with these needs, this is quite some oversight.

In appearing (according to these requirements) to undertake that teaching, the English subject area leaves the students who most need help high and dry; it allows us to believe that the issue of literacy, as the key route to educational success, is actually being dealt with properly in the National Curriculum. And it is not.

Standard English

Instead of literacy, we get Standard English. (Or, rather, 'standard English,' which may or may not be the same thing.) It would be hard to exaggerate just how wrong-headedly this issue is dealt with here.

As is the case throughout, an attempt has been made to represent (re-present, re-cycle, re-tread) ill-informed traditionalist prejudices about correct English in a manner, and in language, which will also be acceptable to the profession (characteristic of the whole process since 1984). No doubt this was viewed as an achievement of sorts by those who wrote the document, achieving compromises comparable to that of enabling the study of media texts so long as they are of high quality. This allows the professionals to tell themselves that they are doing what they believe in, at the same time as flattering the hard-line ideologists of the Right that *they* have finally won the battle to return to the basics of English teaching.

In terms of English, those basics meant more than anything that English teachers were people who knew how to speak and write correctly, and had the nerve to insist that their students did so. It seems so simple, if you see yourself upholding proper and traditional values: teachers should tell children what is right. Every (well-educated) person knows what is right when it comes to the English language – the list is not complicated, or even very long: no prepositions at the end of sentences, no split infinitives, no double negatives, none of those markers of linguistic ignorance such as 'he don't', 'we ain't', or glottal (glo'al) stops. Is that not what *standard* English is after all – a few straightforward prohibitions?

In reality, of course, the new English curriculum document blankly avoids offering any adequate definition of standard English, because it does not have one. Ultimately, anyway, standard English is a concept, not a definition – like love: you know it when it is and is not there, but you cannot actually describe it to someone else, apart from saying that it feels special. Unfortunately, it is also extremely tricky to find the boundaries marking where love and standard English begin and end. For instance, is 'I hate those bloody kids' standard English?

The mistake – which is where the ignorance comes in – is in trying to distinguish between the concepts of *appropriateness* and *correctness*. To the obsessive-traditionalist Right, the English teaching profession's increasing emphasis on the notion of appropriateness instead of correctness since the 1960s seemed to be saying 'do what you like' instead of 'this is right'. In fact, when you give it the smallest amount of objective thought (and the evidence suggests that objective thought has consistently been beyond the scope of the obsessive-traditionalist Right), the notion of appropriateness allows one to say 'this is *right* in *this* situation, and that is *right* in *that* situation'. It is, for instance, always standard English to say 'I hate those bloody kids', but it is not always *appropriate* (as it would not be, for instance, if the Queen began a speech at a Scout display thus). Discussing language in terms of appropriateness results in a far more serious, thoughtful discussion about what is right and wrong than will ever result from the simplistic imposition of correct English. This is sharply illustrated in Geoffrey Leech and Jan Svartvik's very helpful *A Communicative Grammar of English* (nothing wrong with good thinking about grammar, as the LINC project demonstrated). In their section called 'Levels of

Usage: formal and informal English', they provide an invaluable conceptual basis for teaching about language use:

> *Formal* language is the type of language we use publicly for some serious purpose, for example in official reports, business letters, regulations, and academic writing. Formal English is nearly always written, but exceptionally it is used in speech, for example in formal public speeches or lectures.
>
> *Informal* language (also called 'colloquial') is the language of ordinary conversation, of personal letters, and of private interaction in general. It is the first variety of language that a native speaking child becomes familiar with. Because it is generally more accessible to readers or listeners than formal English, it is used more and more nowadays in public communication of a popular kind: for example, in advertisements, popular newspapers, and broadcasting. Informality is typically found in spoken language, although it also occurs quite widely in the written medium, e.g. in diaries, personal letters and popular fiction.
>
> (Leech and Svartvik, 1994: 29)

It is striking that they are able to develop an extremely helpful picture of different levels of formality (and other categories of choice in usage, such as 'Impersonal style', 'Polite and familiar language', 'Tactful and tentative language' and 'Literary, elevated or rhetorical language'; Leech and Svartvik, 1994: 32–4) without recourse to the notion of standard English. At the heart of their exploration of the linguistic features of formal/informal English one finds, instead of dead-end notions of right and wrong in language use, the notion of a continuum:

> The difference between formal and informal usage is best seen as a scale, rather than as a simple 'yes or no' distinction.

They illustrate this scale with the following examples:

- There are many friends to whom one would hesitate to entrust one's own children.
- There are lots of friends you would never trust with your own children.
- There's lots of friends you'd never trust with your own children.
- There's lots of friends you'd never trust with your own kids.

You do not have to be Noam Chomsky to notice the differences here, or even to give names to them. Anyone reading this book could pick out the ways in which those sentences differ, and the different situations in which one would choose those various ways of saying that thing. The fact is, any child in an English classroom could also learn to do this: it is just a question of providing the encouragement and support necessary for articulating intuitive understandings about language usage – thereby advancing considerably towards the crucial goal of exercising choice and control in their own uses of language.

This is what English teaching should provide especially well: opportunities for learning about the choices that can and must be made in the use of language, and help for learners in developing explicit understandings and vision of what *they* can make language do for their own varied and complex needs. The new version of National Curriculum English – unlike the original Cox version – has tried to get by without any vision of English teaching whatsoever, offering instead a set of prescriptions that are the more meaningless and use-less for the attempt to allay liberal anxieties. In a climate of opinion about English teaching that has been increasingly dictated by the combined convic-tions of Rhodes Boyson, Sheila Lawlor, John Marenbon, Prince Charles, David Pascall, John Major, the *Daily Mail* and the *Daily Express*, there is clearly no room for an approach to language learning which allows exploration of, and reflection upon, questions of right and wrong in language use, or which is at all respectful of the learner's own knowledge and needs.

Conclusion

I have said remarkably little about the positive aspects of the new National Curriculum. Of course, there are a lot of decent and sensible suggestions floating around in this document. As a booklet of ideas for English teaching, the new National Curriculum is by no means useless, which after ten years of solid effort, it should not be.

As a curriculum, though, it is not impressive. A curriculum is a means of shaping and balancing what needs to be learnt in a purposeful and progressive way; especially, it must do so in a way that can actually be made to happen. The political tensions and associated muddled thinking which continue to dog the English curriculum have resulted in a design which can contribute very little to the crucial and broad business of helping all our young people to become literate, to meet the full language demands of their lives. Instead we are given a fantasy version of the subject, in which a limited range of highly specialized activities are charged with a task that is way beyond their scope. Most unforgivably, this range of activities is not grounded in reality – neither the reality of the classroom, nor the reality of the students those classrooms serve, nor the reality of the world in which those students live.

4   English for the future

The future has arrived, the landscape is shifting all around us, we are all currently hurtling towards a period of increased and unimaginable change, and meanwhile the education system in England and Wales closes its eyes and dreams of the past. Well, a *bit* exaggerated, perhaps, and not *entirely* fair: but the fact remains that the new curriculum for English is extremely backward-looking. Chapter 3 stated a good deal about the political pressures which helped make our current curriculum so traditionalist, and it really is important not to forget about that degree of influence. It was an ideological, not a natural process: it would be a great mistake to imagine, for instance, that it is necessarily in the *nature* of a National Curriculum to be backward-looking, as a few brief glimpses at what was managed in New Zealand will rapidly demonstrate below.

Indeed, far from there being no actual necessity for a National Curriculum to be dull, safe, and entirely lacking in vision, I would have thought that it was actually the job of education to embrace the present and turn its face towards the future. If you do at all accept the claim with which this chapter begins, that we have all already entered a period of wildly accelerating change, then education ought to be in there, helping to prepare us all. By 'change', I mean both the technological changes which are already having extraordinary kinds of impact on the way we learn, work, exchange goods and money, and live our cultural lives, and the social changes which are so intimately bound up in those technological changes. The world in which our children are growing up is not about to become any less challenging, dangerous, unbalanced or bewildering than it is now. I do not think that our new English curriculum is altogether aware of the nature of social change, or of its own particularly crucial role in helping children become equal to the linguistic and cultural demands of a world in which power is dependent upon the capacity to control communication.

Whilst I am not actually suggesting that the new English curriculum should actually have surfed into our lives over the Internet, or that it should go out of its way to celebrate the post-modernist dislocations of urban breakdown, there clearly is scope for some kind of energetic engagement with the changing culture, values and communicative possibilities which characterize the end of the millennium. I certainly think that, in reflecting upon the nature of English teaching, we should at the very least make every effort to take even further forward its more forward-looking qualities.

English in New Zealand

First of all, I shall try to illustrate my claim that it is possible to conceive of a National Curriculum in general, and an English subject element within that, which reflects and engages with the contemporary world with some vibrancy.

Overall, the New Zealand National Curriculum appears to have benefited considerably from the mistakes made in this country. Whereas Kenneth Baker steadfastly refused to be fooled by the professionals into adopting any kind of imaginative or progressive approach to curriculum design – such as thinking primarily about the different kinds of learning to be ensured (see Chapter 3 and reference to the efforts of HMI in 1985 in this respect) rather than discrete subjects – the New Zealand Government managed to come up with 'a coherent framework for learning and assessment' which 'identifies the essential learning areas and skills'. Figure 4.1 demonstrates the relative adventurousness of their thinking. This chart names both the Essential Learning Areas and the Essential Learning Skills of the curriculum, which schools are encouraged to achieve in whatever ways they choose. It is clear – especially when you look at the Essential Learning Skills – that traditional subject divisions will be called into question by such categories:

> These skills cannot be developed in isolation. They will be developed through the essential learning areas and in different contexts across the curriculum. By relating the development of skills to the contexts in which they are used, both in the classroom and in the wider world, school programmes will provide learning which students can see to be relevant, meaningful, and useful to them.
>
> (New Zealand Ministry of Education, 1993: 17)

Of course, no National Curriculum, however enlightened, can guarantee the successful outcome of such aims, but an underlying structure of this kind might help considerably. Certainly, this more broadly based approach seems better placed to enhance the prospects of successful literacy development than the prevailing situation in the UK.

The English subject requirements within the New Zealand National Curriculum certainly do build on this line of thinking. English is located as a key element in the Essential Learning Area of Language and Languages. The Introduction states:

> Seeking to develop high levels of literacy, the English curriculum . . . establishes language aims for the three 'strands' – oral, written, and visual language.
>
> (New Zealand Ministry of Education, 1994: 6)

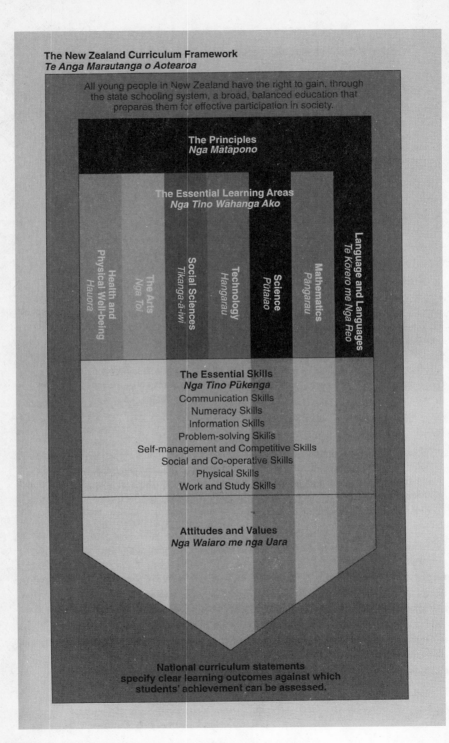

Figure 4.1 The New Zealand Curriculum framework
Te Anga Marautanga o Aotearoa

This is more coherent, more rational and more forward-looking than the method for dividing up the English curriculum adopted in the UK. There is no pretence of dealing with 'Speaking' separately from 'Listening', or 'Writing' separately from 'Reading', there is a recognition of the centrality in young people's lives of visual language, and the whole scheme is directed towards the achievement of 'high levels of literacy'.

The document is not embarrassed or fearful to talk about the social and ideological obligations of English. The requirements and ideas contained within the English curriculum provide concrete examples of how teachers might approach the general New Zealand curriculum requirement that 'All programmes will be gender-inclusive, non-racist, and non-discriminatory, to help ensure that learning opportunities are not restricted.' The following topics from the English subject area indicate the range of classroom possibilities that are envisaged:

- A study of the heritages of the children in the class (students read and talk about the languages, family traditions, and individuals linked to their heritages).
- A language study on gender bias in language (students study and report on language features which they have observed to be gender-marked).
- A class investigation of ways in which language varies according to situation (involves study of different kinds of advertisement).
- Learning about community meetings (includes learning and enacting knowledge of meeting procedures).
- A study of a topical issue, such as health (includes study of strategies for note-taking).
- Developing understanding of a new genre (includes exploration of cues to understanding, and conventions of writing such as text layout, punctuation, etc.).
- Personal storytelling (students move between oral and written storytelling, focusing on ideas from own experience stimulated by teacher's own storytelling).
- A study of the language of film (pupils focus on presentation of characters in film in order to learn about how verbal and visual elements are combined to show meanings).

It is the spread of topics, and the readiness to include perspectives which *ought* to be a normal part of modern life and consciousness, which mark this out so strikingly from the UK version. It is by no means a radical document, and there is still plenty of opportunity and encouragement for the study of poetry, Shakespeare, and the traditional literary-based concerns of English teaching. But neither do the writers seem inhibited by the fear that loud-mouthed, small-minded politicians will restrict necessary kinds of learning with accusations of political correctness or loony Leftism. The New Zealand curriculum – and the new curriculum in Australia achieves much the same, in different ways – simply demonstrates that it is possible to develop and legislate a curriculum which belongs in the present, which in itself now seems like quite an achievement.

Reconceiving the English curriculum

The remainder of this chapter will explore ways of taking what already exists in English – certain practices, opportunities, requirements and realities – and improving on the National Curriculum. This is really not such an ambitious aim. The trick is to get the level of change right: it is relatively easy to come up with visionary schemes for the ideal curriculum (obviously this is what has been attempted, very honourably, in New Zealand), but the real achievement is to envisage and propose changes that are both (a) radical enough to make a difference and (b) close enough to existing reality to be feasible. Given the pressures in schools, and the entirely proper tendency of people to hang on to what they believe in and do well, the scope for fundamentally reconceptualizing the English curriculum is limited, and depends on the making of wise choices about how and exactly what to try to change.

Much as I like the categories of learning in the New Zealand curriculum, and the ways in which these are broken down, I do not think the solution in the UK is actually to burden those doing the job with a whole lot of new concepts, however useful these may be at certain stages in planning and thinking about change. Practitioners are most sympathetic to change which emerges out of practice rather than out of curriculum documents. New categories of learning do not easily take root in people's consciousness (a fact most vividly illustrated by the almost total failure to establish something as necessary and sensible as Language across the Curriculum after the Bullock Report in 1975) and, even with the authority of law, will make little impact on what people actually teach. The way to change what people do is to push forward developments which (often as a result of immense effort by a few determined innovators over many years) have already been quietly established for a while.

In terms of English, I would like to emphasize three aspects of English which should be developed or dealt with differently, in order to achieve the kind of profound and long-term change to the existing balance of the subject which I believe to be essential. These three aspects can broadly be identified as media study, knowledge about language, and general literacy, and are entirely familiar concepts, of course.

I want to argue that the first two of these – media study and knowledge about language – should simply be expanded to constitute one third each of the substantive concerns of the English subject area, with literature study constituting the final third. I then want to argue – and this has been implied all through the preceding chapters – that English should abandon any idea of unique responsibility for teaching general literacy: I want to suggest instead that every effort should always be made to ensure that media study, knowledge about language, and literature study contribute in appropriate and distinctive ways to students' literacy development. Obviously those three areas offer a uniquely focused means of learning about literacy in the way they deal explicitly with language, but there are also many highly important aspects of literacy development which can be dealt with far more effectively elsewhere on the curriculum.

The following sections will go into more detail about the rationale for concentrating differently than at present on each of these areas within the English curriculum.

Media study

As far as I am concerned, the most extraordinary thing that is currently being said about the latest version of the National Curriculum for English is that it allows far more opportunity for studying the media than had been anticipated and, in this respect, is almost as good as the first version of the National Curriculum for English. Which is fine, except that the first version did not actually do all that much to promote media study and had minimal impact on the practice of English teachers and, if this second version is nearly as good, that means it is nothing like good enough.

This is not to suggest that media study as it has so far been constituted is always good or useful, but the modern world, with its extraordinary and exploding communication demands, is an inescapable reality which education overall must engage with – and English does play a crucial part in this. These demands now come at all of us (especially young people, as Peter Benton compellingly demonstrates in Chapter 5) from every possible direction: from the sky, from under the ground, through telephone and electronic networks, from pocket stereos, television, computers and telephones. It is quite extraordinarily blinkered to ignore these things in a curriculum which is expected to take us into the twenty-first century.

The new curriculum provides a few nominal opportunities which the keen and self-motivated teacher of media can take advantage of: in the Key Stages 3 and 4 Programme of Study for Speaking and Listening, one of the range of purposes for talking is 'consideration of ideas, literature and media'; at the same level for Reading, students can 'consider how texts are changed when adapted to different media, e.g. the original text of a Shakespeare play and televised or film versions'; there are brief exemplary suggestions (material in italics being non-statutory) for analysing and evaluating language in a variety of media, 'e.g. . . . a television news bulletin with a report of the same event in a newspaper'; later in the requirements for Writing there is the brief suggestion that out of the extensive range of forms in which students should try to write, could be included 'advertisements and newspaper articles' but the key reference to media study comes, as one might expect, in the Programme of Study for Reading:

Pupils should be introduced to a wide range of media, e.g. magazines, news-papers, radio, television, film. They should be given opportunities to analyse and evaluate such material, which should be of high quality and represent a range of forms and purposes, and different structural and presentational devices.

(HMSO, 1995: 20)

I do not think the proper response to this is to say 'Oh well, at least they've let us do media study', because that is exactly what they have *not* done. The whole point about media study is that it is analytical rather than appreciative or judge-mental. Media study provides a crucial opportunity for developing young people's consciousness of how the technologies of communication and culture influence their lives: by restricting such a perspective to 'high-quality' examples from the popular media, that opportunity is made meaningless and ineffective.

The technologies of communication and culture incorporate both high- and low-level technology: computers, radio, books, TV, worksheets, cinema, theatre, sport, education, newspapers, magazines, posters, street walls. All forms of culture (the processes of communicating beliefs, knowledge, ideas and values within different social groups) from graffiti to Sky TV, from *Viz* to the Royal Shakespeare Company, from Ingmar Bergman to *Gladiators* are potential ob-jects of attention. Some of these things fill children's lives; some do not touch them at all: but all children ought to be given the resources to cope with the impact each of these might have on what they think about the world.

I think that an educational ideology which prevents teachers from preparing young people to cope on equal terms with all that is pouring into their con-sciousness from the world around them is more wicked than ignorant. The following statement of intent for media study is an attempt to formulate the basis upon which (I think) the media *should* be studied:

Statement of intent for media study

Media study should look at how meanings about the world are:

- made
- sustained
- contested

in *all* forms of human communication. It should study *what* those meanings and beliefs are, *where* they come from, *who* makes them and *why*.

This kind of English operates on the principles that:

- the more those forms or media influence us (by determining our thinking and actions) the more we should study them;
- the more we benefit from them (by gaining understanding, and means of expression) the more we should learn how to use them positively;
- it is not the job of media study to teach people what the right meanings are, or what the right pleasures are – its particular task is to teach people to examine how meanings are made.

Now I do realize that there are only so many times one can say the word 'meanings' before it becomes totally meaningless, so some examples might be in order.

For instance, one very influential set of 'meanings' which media of all kinds make and sustain concern understandings about the worth of different kinds of people, according to categories such as race, nationality, class and gender. I know that conservative common sense has tried to convince us in recent years that such categories are no longer relevant, but one only needs to switch on a TV to discover certain clearly defined and unvarying relationships between identity and value. There is a lot to be learnt by questioning whether it is *really* the case that middle-class, middle-aged, white men in suits know most about how the world works, or whether the only good woman is a pretty one, or whether black people are ever bad at sport or rhythm, or whether people from Liverpool are ever prim and humourless.

Such a perspective focuses on the role played by different media, and the techniques used within those media, in maintaining or strengthening the social ideologies that make life work smoothly for some, and unfairly for others. In addition, media study allows us to focus on other fundamental issues such as the role played by various kinds of media in teaching us who to vote for, how to spend our money and what our moral laws should be. The unique quality of media study in respect of such things (which could also be studied through literary study, but in quite different ways) is its capacity to expose the workings of ideology below the surfaces of normality. That is an exciting kind of study, and qualitatively different from literary appreciation, which teaches us to ask 'what is this writer trying to reveal about that big question?' – media study teaches us to ask 'what message is this text trying to *hide* about that big question?'

Sometimes the hiding is absolute, as in the negative information about who has power in society (TV knows how to keep the powerless quiet, not seen and not heard), and when any kind of debate between different interest groups occurs, the medium itself controls the terms of engagement. Consider, for instance, the following exchange (provided by Len Masterman in *Teaching the Media*) following the infamous riot at Orgreave during the UK miners' strike in 1984 (a riot which some attributed to the miners and others to the police): TV interviewer Nick Ross very clearly indicates where authority lies in the way he introduces the representatives of the two sides of the battle. First was Jack Taylor from the National Union of Mineworkers:

> *Nick Ross:* Mr Taylor, how on earth do you explain what happened at Orgreave today?

After that interview, Nick Ross turned to Eldon Griffiths, Tory MP, and Parliamentary Spokesman for Police Federation, and asked (Masterman, 1985: 119–120):

> *Nick Ross:* You heard that Mr Griffiths – what is your assessment of what happened today?

'How on earth?' instantly tells us not to trust the answer, just as 'what is your assessment?' confers credibility and respect. Obviously Nick Ross himself would strenuously deny any such intention but then this has nothing to do with his *intention* anyway, because seen from the media study perspective we need only view him as a functionary in a meaning-making process. Media study is not about whether people do things well or badly (the perspective implied by the notion of 'high-quality' texts) so much as it is about the far larger meaning-making processes which subsume all those people's individual intentions and talents.

It should be possible at this stage, and it would certainly be helpful, to clarify things somewhat: I am using 'literary study' and 'media study' simply as technical terms for certain teaching and learning activities whose conceptual foundations would take rather too long to state each time, if we had to encode them more accurately in their titles (of course, other and better names for these activities would ideally be helpful, but because people adopt change quite slowly and reluctantly it is probably simpler to appropriate existing names):

- Literary study. This term is used here to stand for the study and exploration of the complexities, subtleties and insights of good and worthwhile texts (what the National Curriculum means by 'high quality'); these could quite logically include both traditional and modern texts, any of which could quite reasonably be enjoyed on the page, in the theatre, in the cinema, or on TV. An essential element of such study is pupils' own production of texts that are broadly literary (imaginative, reflective, carefully crafted).
- Media study. This term stands for the study and analysis of any texts that exemplify communicative processes, such as those which sustain ideology; these texts can be different from or the same as those studied under the previous heading of literary study – it is the purposes of this study that are quite different. This study also requires the pupils to attempt the production of similar types of text.

Every kind of text is potentially revealing of the relationship between communicative process and meaning-making, whether it is a deliberate and targeted meaning-making (such as in advertising), something more subtly concealed, or something that is not necessarily even consciously perpetrated. The latter is very nicely instanced in a light-hearted look, in the rock magazine *Select*, at certain conventions of the cinema. Headed 'Marked for Death', this article's clever little study of 'How to spot who's going to get theirs in the movies!' actually demonstrates very vividly how something as apparently empty and insignificant as the narrative conventions of a cop movie actually represents a major part of the social process of agreeing and reminding ourselves about certain moral laws. The article asks: 'Are they smoking? Cruel to kids? Shagging around? Snorting loads of cocaine? Then they're DEAD MEAT. Clark Collis presents the Definitive Rules of Death on the Silver Screen . . .', and quotes a range of reasons why certain characters are always doomed to die in certain kinds of drama – rules that tell us both about technical knowledge needed to follow the plot of a movie and about the social norms which mainstream entertainment so piously reinforces. The article goes on to advise:

> **Be a coward**. Death guaranteed. **Be cruel to kids or animals. Be fat, smoke or otherwise transgress healthy-living norms**. All the self-neglecters in *Jurassic Park* get chomped (Spielberg cast Wayne Knight after his top performance as a greaseball in *Basic Instinct*, purely because he was fat).
>
> (*Select* Magazine, May 1993)

But it is not just a matter of media study bringing to the surface the hidden, or the unintentional. Deliberate, targeted *and* explicit meaning-making also needs to be studied closely, for the important reason – as is obviously the case with advertising, for instance – that just because we know and can see the *sort* of thing that is going on, that still does not mean that we are fully aware of or equal to the way it is being done. This is a case of: 'Dammit, these guys are always one step ahead! We've really got to *struggle* to keep up with them!'

A perfect instance of this are the various stunning attacks on the Labour Party which *The Sun* has mounted during recent General Elections. Nobody was in any doubt that headlines like 'Will the Last One to Leave the Country Please Turn Out the Lights?' and its jokey terror announcement that Neil Kinnock had won, the day before the actual election, were never intended to be read as other than spoofs, and yet even so the audience had no choice but to take them seriously. This is because of far more subtle strategies at work below the surface, such as the longer-term process of characterizing Kinnock as fool, day in and day out, and creating the demons of the loony Left. Specially memorable in this process was the trick, used in both the 1987 and 1992 General Elections, of one morning during the campaign presenting Page 3 with a blank white space where the topless *Sun* girl should have been, and explaining that this was what 'The Soaraway *Sun*' would be like every day, if the Labour Party got elected (Figure 4.2). Regardless of a quiet retraction the next day – presumably at the insistence of an appalled Labour Party – the damage was done. This was a pretty crude trick, but it must have hurt the Labour Party a good deal, simply because of the longer term process of meaning-making which that one brilliant rhetorical flourish of a blank page drew upon.

Mark Pursehouse, from the Birmingham University Centre for Contemporary Cultural Studies, reveals just how powerful that rhetorical flourish was in one of the interviews he carried out with *Sun* readers (all of whom proved to be articulate and thoughtful commentators on their own processes of reading, which rather disposes of the notion the *Sun*'s methods work simply because its readers are 'thick'). He is talking to Adrian, a twenty-year old from the Midlands, who works for a local building company as a qualified bricklayer.

Figure 4.2 'The loveliest girls *were* in *The Sun*'. Press scare tactics – vote Labour, no Page 3 girl

Mark: Describe what you do on your working day.

Adrian: Well, it consists of getting up around 6.45. Down at work for 7 o'clock . . . arriving there, unlocking, going to the cabin, having a quick cup of tea and a glance at the paper. At this stage only the back page. . . . That's the first look of the day – not even when I buy it – I've got to be in the cabin first. Then it's never opened – it's only the back page, due to the quick rush of having a quick cup of tea and going straight out – just a quick read.

Mark: Is there another look at the paper at breakfast?

Adrian: Yes we do. We get to breakfast; at this stage it's straight to the highlight of the day, turning to Page 3. Just a quick glance like opening it up – never before. If anybody asks me 'what's on Page 3?' which some do like, in the morning as soon as we get there, I always open it and never show me, so they can see and they'll comment – I don't look myself. Very, er, specific point that is to save that till breakfast.

(Pursehouse, 1987)

If turning to Page 3 has become a sort of highlight of the day for a hard-pressed working man, then the deliberate removal of that is more than just a crude attack on Left-wing political correctness, it is also a stupendous rhetorical flourish, playing ruthlessly on well-known and well-established expectations of the readers. It is the manipulation of a convention for a purpose.

I do not think therefore that it is adequate to see media study as simply helping young people to learn how to name, recognize and reproduce the conventions and techniques of various visual and verbal media, any more than it is media study if you simply use a particular medium such as TV for watching a Shakespeare play, or seeing a documentary on the environment. As far as media study is concerned, the study of conventions, processes and issues is purposeful only insofar as it heightens understanding and awareness of how all kinds of media influence our beliefs about who we are and how we ought to behave.

Of course, it is fun to bring our innate knowledge of the media to the surface, and it is true that a lot of us just enjoy talking about last night's TV programmes, the movies we have seen, what is in the paper, good adverts, and so on. There might be a temptation, therefore, to engage with media study activities in the hope that students will enjoy it more than *Romeo and Juliet*, or because it provides good material for broadly desirable English activities like small group discussion, or the exploration of personal feelings or current issues. But I am suggesting here that the rationale for media study must be tougher and more focused, for two inseparable reasons: (i) students often feel quite uncomfortable studying the texts of popular culture in the classroom, and come to believe that the only texts worth analysing or studying seriously are those they do not actually enjoy, unless (ii) it can be demonstrated that there are indeed important reasons for doing this.

Richard Dyer presents a particularly lucid argument for the study of popular texts (whether high quality or not) in an article entitled 'Taking Popular

Television Seriously'. In this extract he explores four different ways of using the term 'representation', as a means of demonstrating the kinds of perspectives that media study has to offer. He starts by discussing 'representation' as 're-presentation', i.e. presenting reality over again:

> 'Representation' insists that there is a real world, but that our perception of it is always mediated by television's selection, emphasis and use of technical/aesthetic means to render that world to us. . . . there is no perception of the world except one that is mediated through the forms of representation available in the culture, of which television is one of the most powerful. . . .
>
> Secondly, 'representation' suggests the function of 'being representative of'. In other words, it raises the question of *typicality*. To what extent are representations of men and women, whites and blacks, different classes etc. typical of how those groups are in society?
>
> Thirdly, there is representation in the sense implied in the Representation of the People Act, that is, in the sense of *speaking for and on behalf of*. This is where the most political heat is generated because, faced with television images, we constantly need to ask not 'What is this image of?' so much as 'Who is speaking here?' For every image of a woman, it is important to ask who is speaking for women at that point. In the vast majority of cases, the answer would be a man. The same is true of other groups excluded from the mainstream of speech in our society. Television so often speaks on our behalf without letting us speak for ourselves.
>
> Finally, representation should also make us think of the *audience*. In this inflection, we should include ourselves: what does this programme represent to me; what does it mean to other people who watch it? We often leave this stage out of account; especially, I regret to say, in education. Teachers often try to get pupils and students to see what a programme represents 'ideally' (i.e. as teachers understand it) without also finding out what it represents to them.
>
> (Dyer, 1983: 44–5)

Media study is not just about modern media, or popular texts, of course. Books are unambiguously to be included in any adequate notion of the media, and that includes literature. Books have the advantage of being easy to study (they tend to sit accessibly on the desk), but technology is now making the detailed and analytical study of all kinds of media feasible in schools, and even quite basic computers now can provide opportunities for video capture, whereby one can freeze any image from a video tape and either print it out (in a worksheet), or include it as a quote in an essay. Computers also make it possible to edit video cheaply and easily, and communications systems like Internet mean that one can share images and meanings, for good or ill, around the world, and instantly.

None of this is in the National Curriculum, but that need not stand in our way.

Knowledge about language

The term 'knowledge about language' has exercised English teachers' thinking since 1984 when *English from 5 to 16* was published, through the Kingman

Report, the Cox Reports and the first version of the National Curriculum for English which they produced, LINC (the Language in the National Curriculum project) and beyond. At the peak of its importance, between 1989 and 1991, it gave birth to so many attempts at clarification that it rather began to explain itself out of existence. Since then the Government has tried its best to complete that process by replacing 'knowledge about language' as a category of the English curriculum with 'standard English and language study' which – given the fact that the hard-line revisionists were apparently pushing hard for 'grammar' – represents another of those clever compromises for which we are supposed to be so grateful.

Knowledge about language appeared to provide an opening both for the prescriptivist approach to teaching about language that the Government thought it wanted and for the more analytical, descriptivist approach that professionals favoured. This is why the Government funded LINC in the first place, as Chapter 3 explained: it wanted someone to come up with a clear taxonomy of knowledge about how to write and speak properly that would, if successfully inserted into students' heads, actually ensure that they did write and speak properly. The professionals knew that teaching people to use language success-fully is more complicated than that, but were willing to play along in order to keep the bosses happy, especially because this allowed them to introduce a more analytical kind of language study into the English subject area at the same time.

The second Cox Report (*English for Ages 5 to 16*, June 1989, DES) came up with what sounded like an acceptable formula to support this particular accommodation:

> Two justifications for teaching pupils explicitly about language are, first, the positive effect on aspects of their use of language and secondly, the general value of such knowledge as an important part of their understanding of their social and cultural environment, since language has vital functions in the life of the indi-vidual and society.
>
> (DES, 1989: para. 6.7)

According to this, knowledge about language is important both because (a) it contributes in some way to the process of learning to use language and (b) it provides students with other kinds of valuable knowledge about the world they live in. It followed that the term 'knowledge about language' could refer both to *explicit* and *implicit* knowledge about language, and that with any luck knowledge about the former might contribute directly to the latter (given that, really, implicit knowledge about language meant the ability to *use* language well). The next thing we knew, it turned out that *everything* in English amounted, when you thought about it, to knowledge about language.

Unfortunately, this whole accommodation went badly wrong. First of all, the Government noticed that LINC was definitely not providing a taxonomy of right and wrong: on the contrary, it was advocating subversion, such as training teachers to deconstruct the speeches of Mrs Thatcher. Even with the funding stopped, though, knowledge about language remained part of the National Curriculum, which turned out to be both good news and bad news. The good news was obviously that the struggle to develop this interesting and important new strand of English could continue; the bad news was that the tendency to use the term to refer to *everything* in English resulted in a loss of momentum in agreeing a clear and purposeful agenda for teaching an *explicit* knowledge about language.

In the end, it is therefore not bad news, I think, that the revised National Curriculum has dumped the term, because that allows us to reclaim and re-energize it somewhat. Admittedly, some of the topics included in the original curriculum as knowledge about language do still remain, but the logic of their inclusion has very little to do with increasing students' *knowledge* (as something which ideally provides the basis for autonomous choice). For instance, whilst it is the case that this document does say that 'Pupils should be given opportunities . . . to distinguish varying degrees of formality, selecting appropriately for a task', it is only actually saying you can choose anything you like, so long as it is standard English:

> 3 Standard English and Language Study
> (a) Pupils should be encouraged to be confident in the use of formal and informal written standard English, using the grammatical, lexical and orthographic features of standard English, except where non-standard forms are required for effect or technical reasons.

And that is as open-minded as it gets. Beyond that, it is pure sophistry, saying for instance that students should be given opportunities for reflection and analysis, in order that they might find out where they have broken the rules of standard English:

> (b) Pupils should be encouraged to broaden their understanding of the principles of sentence grammar and be taught to organise whole texts effectively. Pupils should be given opportunities to analyse their own writing, reflecting on the meaning and clarity of individual sentences, using appropriate terminology, and so be given opportunities to learn about:
>
> ● discourse structure . . .
> ● phrase, clause and sentence structure . . .
> ● words . . .
> ● punctuation . . .

(DFE, 1995a: 24)

It is interesting to see how vestiges of the Cox curriculum have been appropriated in order to provide further criteria for prescriptions on correctness. This is particularly inappropriate in the case of 'discourse analysis', a form of knowledge about language which asks only 'What are the internal rules determining the choices made in this instance of writing (or speech)?' In exploring the answers to such a question, it would be meaningless for discourse analysis to be concerned with *general* values of correctness, neatness or good paragraphing. You could take a piece of writing by William Burroughs, a monologue from Tommy Cooper, or a rant from Prince Charles and discover all sorts of internal rules of cohesion and coherence, none of which need necessarily be externally correct, in terms of standard English: that would not make those rules any less interesting, or any less revealing of the relationship between function and feature in that particular case.

The understanding of such a perspective on language represents very well, in effect, why it is worth developing the study of an explicit, linguistics-based knowledge about language. This would in effect be a fundamentally scholarly study of how language works. To be worthwhile, such study must be concerned exclusively with truthful and non-judgemental accounts of language, which will not be the case if such study is distorted in order to provide additional opportunities for teaching students not to break language etiquette. The point is that *both* these things are necessary and feasible aims for teaching young people: *of course* young people should be taught how not to break language etiquette, because of the terrible judgements visited upon them when they do, but it is equally the case that they are capable of, and will benefit from, academic study (they do it in other subjects, such as history, geography, science, etc. where presumably not *every* act of learning is intended to lead to direct changes in behaviour).

It might be the case that in the long run, learning about how language works will enable learners to make what are generally considered to be desirable choices about language use, but the extent to which they refer to that knowledge in making those choices is unpredictable; some of that knowledge might provide good reasons for breaking language etiquette on occasions. It might turn out to be the case that, for example, having learnt the history of Standard English they come to realize how history, power relations and linguistic processes have forced them to adopt language manners which they now see as oppressive. That is up to them: as I stated earlier, it is the function of knowledge to provide a firm basis for autonomous decisions. Somewhat less acceptable is the distortion of knowledge in order to direct people's behaviour, which is what the National Curriculum requirements actually seem to be doing at times.

Teaching knowledge about language

The preceding argument has been necessary in order to try to clear some space in our thinking, and on the English curriculum, for the study of *explicit* knowledge about the English language. This is an important and relevant area, but no-one can really say whether this will directly improve children's language skills; their *literacy*. But then, no-one really knows whether the study of literature can do that either (although claims of this kind are constantly made in justification for the study of literature). I think that, like studying literature, explicit knowledge about language adds to young people's understanding about the world, on a dimension that is obviously not trivial. And, like literature, it logically belongs in the subject called 'English'.

There have been a number of valuable attempts to detail a programme for the study of knowledge about language, notably of course in the Cox reports and subsequently in LINC, and there are also a number of important related texts which explore exciting possibilities for such teaching in detail (see Bibliography). I will not try here either to develop a comprehensive programme for knowledge about language, or provide teaching ideas: one would need a whole book, and *then* some, for each of these purposes. Instead, I shall simply present the main topics that constitute what I mean by 'explicit knowledge about language', in order simply to demonstrate my claim that this is an authentic and coherent area of study, with a real claim to its own space in the English curriculum.

Here, first of all, is an overview of the topics, in one possible (out of many) logical order, for a programme of study that would last the whole of compulsory secondary education at least:

- The history of the English language:
    the development of dialects of English
    the development of standard English
    language change
- Language structures: an introduction to descriptive linguistics
- The nature of language variation:
    variation according to user: social class and locality
    variation according to use: register (discourse analysis)
    attitudes to language variation
- Language development and learning
- Language and power: gender, race, class and education.

The study of the beginnings of the English language would demonstrate, first of all, that language is a historical rather than merely natural fact (the product of invasion, imperialism and conflict). It might also make clear that there was never anything particularly English about English. From this basis, one can move on to the discovery that the most artificial kind of language of all is the standard form (despite the belief of some that standard English is somehow the proper God-given version of the language).

In respect of standard English, it is worth checking the chapter in the Penguin collection *Sociolinguistics* (Haugen, 1972) which outlines the key stages in the development of standard English as selection, acceptance, codification, elaboration. This is, after all, a historically describable, rather than a mystical, process – remarkably similar, in fact, to the establishment of Association Football in the mid-nineteenth century, whereby a group of boys at Oxbridge, all from privileged boarding schools, agreed on a set of rules for the game by which everyone else would have to abide. Not altogether amazingly, standard English originates from that same south Midlands triangle of Oxford, Cambridge and London.

The study of the development of standard English will provide the basis for the study, later on, of issues such as language variation (how come different versions of the same language continue to survive in different parts of the country, and in different social classes, after all these years?) and attitudes to variation (how come some forms of language make people seem more clever and more important than others?). Before they get to that, though, students can begin to learn ways of naming and talking about language, in the process of learning its structures – as soon as they start to name different bits and pieces of language structure, they are in a position to start relating knowledge of language forms to function (such as reflecting on why glottal stopping should be such a satisfactory means of earning the disapproval of parents and teachers).

The final key element in the process is the development of awareness about register (or genre, or discourse), which reveals the internal rules of different language forms that enable people to produce and recognize different uses of language straightaway. Such understandings arise directly out of the combination of an awareness of language variation, and a growing ability to name the structures of language: on such a basis it is not difficult to begin to identify the distinctive linguistic features of anything from teenage slang, to *Sun* headlines or a teacher's tirade. The ability to articulate such things is absolutely at the heart of knowledge about language.

There is no limit to the scope for increased sophistication in such study over the years, so that eventually students can find themselves asking and investigating profound questions about the relationships between language and power in society, and the role of education (including their own education) in that process. Interestingly, these forms of study come nearer than anything previously part of the English subject area – with the exception of the old study of the rules and terminology of Latinate grammar – to a solid and detailed knowledge base for the subject. What separates them from Latinate grammar is the way this kind of sociolinguistic knowledge base also relates to the real social world that young people experience all the time.

The knowledge about language that is being proposed here is entirely and unambiguously explicit – that is its beauty and its value, because the more precise we are about what we are trying to teach, the greater hope of teaching it effectively. This part of the English timetable sets up opportunities to learn how to talk about and describe the English language, and to see that language as an entity with a specific history and specific characteristics *as a language*. This involves the study of the English language, and not the study of how to use it, which must occur systematically on a far wider base than is currently catered for in our curriculum.

General literacy

Obviously the knowledge about language that has been outlined above has a great deal to contribute to literacy development, and in certain respects – such as explicit teaching about language structures – comes closest to popular views of how that development happens. At the risk of labouring this point, I would rather say that knowledge about language does not offer all that much directly towards the development of literacy, even in its concentration on language structures: it is unlikely that knowledge of the structural characteristics of a sentence can actually help the majority of people to write a good sentence in their own language; at most, it might help a teacher to talk to a learner about things that have been left out. It is just as likely (and likely guesses are all we have to go on in this respect) that the most useful guidance is simply to help learners articulate their own intuitions about sentences, supported by a few obvious and simple rules about what to do then: whenever you think you have written a sentence, make sure you start with a capital letter and end with a full stop. All three aspects of English (media study, knowledge about language, literature study, as I am proposing here) have an immense contribution to make to the development of literacy. Because of the explicit interest in language upon which each of these three strands of the subject depends, and which presumably all English teachers share, this specialist contribution will inevitably be far greater than any other single subject can make. It seems not unreasonable to suggest that this contribution can be made in the following ways, some unique to English, and some shared with other subjects:

1 The experience of extended reading.
2 Reflection upon language as an observable and rule-governed phenomenon.
3 The experience of several key forms of writing, both as reader and writer: poetic, imaginative, self-expressive, descriptive, analytical, argumentative, evaluative.
4 The experience of a variety of spoken language opportunities.

There is no need to be absolutely precise about where the uniqueness ends and the shared contribution begins, but it is certainly interesting and informative to look a little more closely at what seems to be the distinctive contributions of English to this list.

The first item on the above list probably is unique to English. Certainly English has traditionally provided richer opportunities than other subjects for sustained and reflective reading, which according to one influential study (Lunzer and Gardner, 1979) is a crucial aspect in the successful development of reading skills. English teachers have often tended, and over recent years increasingly so, to provide dedicated opportunities both for the extended reading, and for supported reflection upon that reading (the importance of which is re-emphasized by Peter Benton in Chapter 5).

The second of these, i.e. knowledge about language, is nearly but not quite

unique to English, given that modern languages teaching also can and sometimes does help students reflect on similar issues, although obviously not
specifically in relation to the English language. This area has in fact frequently
turned out to be a doomed meeting-place between the two subjects, leading
to more in the way of mutual recrimination than any productive harnessing
of shared concerns. Certainly, if an English teacher wants to get students to
reflect on technical aspects of their own language, it can help considerably to
direct their attention to the strangeness of another language, just as the familiarity of English can sometimes be useful for the modern languages teacher as
a means of defusing that strangeness.

Some kinds of writing out of the list given in the third item above, such as
poetic, imaginative and self-expressive, are likely to be experienced exclusively
– or at any rate, predominantly – in English. These are the kinds of writing
which allow us to reflect on and express one's life and feelings, whether auto-
biographically or imaginatively: as English teachers have also always claimed,
this really is something unique to the subject. I simply want to formulate that
uniqueness in terms of it being a *unique contribution to developing literacy*
(described in Chapter 3 as 'the reading and writing skills that you need in life')
that English teaching can make, as important as – but not necessarily more
important than – the other kinds of contribution which other kinds of subject
can uniquely provide (such as history's unique emphasis on locating, reading,
recording, evaluating and synthesizing documentary evidence).

In addition, the kinds of writing that English shares with other subjects –
descriptive, analytical, argumentative, evaluative – are no less important for
being shared. The increasing emphasis on the analytic work arising out of
media study and knowledge about language, for instance, should ensure a rapid
expansion of that area of the subject's contribution to general literacy, and
English teachers should embrace that opportunity also: with the same conscious and deliberate emphasis on the actual literacy skills involved as teachers
of all subjects must learn to make.

I would suggest that English has nothing *unique* whatsoever to offer oracy
development, although it does of course *share* with all other subjects a very
crucial role in developing skills and habits of spoken language use. Hopefully,
there is no single spoken language opportunity which could not usefully occur
in all subjects, including scripted or improvised drama (which, as any specialist
drama teacher will tell you, is by no means either the prerogative of English
teachers, or even something they are particularly good at).

It is clear that English does have some very special contributions to make to
the development of literacy. Above all, English is a subject for people who *love*
language, and it is a good bet that a love of language is a big factor in
becoming effectively and successfully literate. But all the undoubtedly unique
contributions that it has to make to literacy are no more important, ultimately,
than the contributions which it shares with other subjects. And the fact is that
the specialism of English offers *no* greater opportunities than any other subject

for many crucial aspects of literacy development, such as learning to handwrite legibly, read methodically, spell accurately, write for specific audiences, or use the written and spoken word for recording, organizing, analysing, synthesizing and discussing information and knowledge. Not, that is, if along with me you accept the claim – upon which this whole argument is contingent – that *people only learn things in purposeful and meaningful contexts.* That is to say, for example, that people *only* learn to write notes properly when they have an authentic and felt need to write notes. Or that people only learn how to win an argument, in speech or writing, when that argument means something to them. So long as the English curriculum is charged with the task of providing general and transferable literacy skills, then it will find itself teaching techniques of language that mean nothing to learners, cobbling together false concerns and phoney information as dry runs for activities which take place elsewhere in the curriculum anyway. The result of this will be that some children – a large slice of the population – will simply never learn these skills, because they will not be taught when they are most needed.

Naturally, all this will (as ever) disadvantage the most disadvantaged. This, I think, is because the eventual success of some children in developing literacy allows us to believe that literacy is being actively and systematically taught in schools. In this line of thinking, the failure of a number of students (I am not guessing here what proportion that is, but any at all is too many) to develop adequate levels of general literacy before they leave school can only be explained in terms of the lack of some innate capacity for which schools cannot hope to compensate. A more convincing argument would suggest that the success of some and the failure of others in this respect is because those who succeed have privileged access to sufficient educational and linguistic resources elsewhere (parental involvement, linguistic and educational background) to compensate for what is not systematically taught in school. Schools must see themselves as fully responsible for the language and literacy development of all students. Ultimately, therefore, the question of literacy is one which sees good teaching synonymous with educational justice, because good teaching ensures successful learning for everyone.

The role of English teaching in all this is to recognize what it can and cannot contribute to this crucial process. By attempting less than it currently attempts, it can achieve more: by getting on with what it can do well and appropriately, at the same time as making clear what the responsibilities of other areas of the curriculum are in this respect, English teaching and English teachers can significantly advance the essential cause of general literacy for all.

Conclusion

This chapter claims to provide a vision of an English curriculum which looks to the future; which will take us into the next century. Really, though, this is not about the English teaching that ought to happen in five years time (schools will not last for ever, anyway): this chapter is about the English we ought to be teaching today. There is nothing suggested here which is not to some extent already happening in a great many schools – it is really a question of conceptualizing a subject out of existing practices and beliefs that is more appropriate to the needs of all our students than that conceptualized in the National Curriculum.

I am suggesting here that the English curriculum should abandon pious and unrealistic claims for teaching general literacy, and therefore can give up its current unhelpful and uninspiring methods for categorizing and managing the subject. Instead, English should focus in more tightly and more realistically on the already complex and varied contributions which it provenly can make to young people's lives in terms of their literacy and culture, by dealing *in equal measure* with the following three areas:

- Media: the study and production of cultural and linguistic forms in terms of how they influence and determine one's view and experience of the world.
- Knowledge about language: the close study of language as a medium in itself; the most crucial medium in any human's life.
- Literature: the study and production of cultural and linguistic forms in terms of aesthetic, emotional and humane values.

In so doing, English will both have a greater chance of actively and *appropriately* helping young people to become properly literate, and will finally get on with the task – which it so patently ought to have done something about by now – of becoming that aspect of education which can help people deal with a cultural world that is currently advancing and changing at the speed of light.

5 Children's reading and viewing in the nineties

PETER BENTON

In this chapter, Peter Benton draws on his own current research in order to paint an exceptionally vivid picture of the varied and demanding cultural world inhabited by the young people that English teaching today aims to engage with and educate.

The National Curriculum at Key Stages 3 and 4 requires that students should be 'given access to significant authors and works from the English literary heritage' and be 'introduced to major works of literature from the English literary heritage in previous centuries' (DFE, 1995a: 19). They should also 'read literature by major writers from earlier in the twentieth century and works of high quality by contemporary writers' (DFE, 1995a: 19). The words 'major' and 'high quality' run through the text like a refrain, and the lists of approved novelists, dramatists and poets drive home the message that this is a *national* curriculum which has little time for anything that was not already a part of the established canon of over 30 years ago; it celebrates predominantly the word of the dead, white, male. True, there is a belated recognition of multi-cultural literature for its offering of 'distinctive voices and forms' and 'varied perspectives and subject matter' and of media – magazines, newspapers, radio, television and film – but even here such material 'should be of high quality'. Rhodes Boyson's unashamedly nationalist, traditionalist and commonsensically élitist stance with regard to literature set out as long ago as 1975 (subsequently underwritten and promulgated by the National Curriculum) states that:

> About 100 texts in literature should be laid down of which it would be expected that every student covered some 40 books and plays. There is no common culture without a basic literature and without this the country could fall apart.
>
> The choice of books can range from R.L. Stevenson, Kipling, Dickens, Jane Austen, the Brontës up to 1984, *Lord of the Flies* and recent classics. Passing fashions of taste have no place in basic school teaching. Two or three of the easier Shakespeare plays should be included.
>
> (Boyson, 1975)

And so, in 1995, it came to pass.

The National Curriculum also continually stresses a view of literature as having a moral force, with a thrice repeated injunction laid upon teachers to choose plays, novels and poems that will 'extend students' ideas and their moral and emotional understanding' (DFE, 1995a: 19).

Yet for all this direction, the National Curriculum insists that students should also be 'given opportunities to read a wide variety of literature. They should also be encouraged 'to read widely and independently solely for enjoyment' and 'the main emphasis should be on the encouragement of wider reading in order to develop independent, responsive and enthusiastic readers' (DFE, 1995a: 19).

Given that these are stated goals of the National Curriculum with regard to reading, it is interesting and helpful to see them in the context of what students *actually* read, by free choice, when reading 'independently solely for enjoyment'. And given that all such reading takes place against a background of – and to some extent in competition with – other texts such as television programmes and computer games, it is helpful to have some knowledge of what adolescents actually choose to watch on their screens.

A key question is whether teachers should promulgate only the heritage model of the National Curriculum ignoring that which may be read by students but is clearly not of 'high quality'. Given that there is at least some mention of understanding media in the National Curriculum, the question may be extended further to ask whether or not the student's *viewing* habits have an effect upon reading or, whether indeed they are a proper area of study.

Teachers will be at a disadvantage in understanding their students' responses to reading and to literature unless they have at least some understanding of, and interest in, the reading and viewing culture that adolescents are busily constructing and reconstructing in their everyday lives. Official texts are read in the context of a multitude of unofficial texts both literary and visual. There is no reason to believe that such unofficial texts are any less important in shaping students' imaginative capacity and view of the world than those promulgated by the formal demands of the curriculum. Indeed it may be in tacit recognition of this point that the National Curriculum is deliberately set up in opposition to what may be regarded as the ephemera of modern media: if English teachers do not offer great literature, it may be claimed, students will never know what it has to offer.

Teachers, particularly those who feel they have gained significant personal insights from their study of literature, sometimes tend to assume a shared set of values exists between them and their students with regard to literary texts: it is not uncommon to discover that this assumption may be misplaced. What in Boyson's terms, is 'the common culture' without which 'the country could fall apart' is perhaps represented not so much by Dickens or Shakespeare but much more by *Neighbours* and *Eastenders*, by the *Sun* and *Just 17*, Judy Blume and R.T. Cusick. Whether we like it or not, these are the words students choose to read, these are the images students choose to see and it is surely patronizing and ultimately foolish to suggest that they are of no account and unworthy of serious study.

They matter for very practical reasons of teachers' practice in choosing and using texts in schools and in developing students' attitudes to reading and towards film and television. Texts offered from on high without an understanding of students' own reading and viewing background are likely to be rejected. A rejection by the teacher of student culture may not only encourage a rejection of the teacher's culture by the students, it also rejects a potentially valuable area of study and engagement. Charles Sarland's *Young People Reading: Culture and Response* (1991) and *Un/popular Fictions* (Moss, 1989) usefully explore different aspects of this view. Attitudes and opinions are shaped by *Smash Hits* as much if not more than by Brontë or Blake and these views will be developed in class discussion and in the stories students tell and write. A concern only for 'high quality' in terms of media study must appear unreal to students and of course, as in all the other cases where that phrase is used, it begs the question of who is the arbiter of quality and upon what grounds.

Without some knowledge of the facts of students' self-chosen reading and viewing, we are reliant upon myth and prejudice. For example, concern over reading standards is often related, rightly or wrongly to the amount of time spent watching television and playing video games – the implication being that children become fluent readers by practice and that television viewing not only takes from the time available for mastering and enjoying the skill but presents an altogether different and, some would claim, an inferior, more passive experience. It has become the accepted folk wisdom that children do not read any more, that they just sit around watching television or playing computer games. But, as Gillian Cross points out:

> Of course children watch television and play with computers: we should be grateful that they adjust so readily to new devices. But there is no reason to think that they do these things instead of reading . . . The comprehensive public library statistics compiled by the Library and Information Statistics Unit at Loughborough University show, quite unmistakably, that, while borrowing by adults has declined over the past few years, the number of books on loan to children has actually increased.
>
> (Cross, 1995)

As Cross remarks, literacy has become a political battleground and there are factions who are determined to convince the public that standards have fallen. Claim follows counter claim, but the truth is that we simply do not know enough to have a clear view on this issue.

Concerns about reading and viewing

As a child's experience of school is very largely a linguistic experience requiring increasing sophistication in terms of reading, writing and comprehension skills, anything which reduces engagement with the printed word could be seen as reducing development in these areas. Indeed it has been suggested that the well-documented phenomenon of boys reading less than girls as they progress through adolescence may have been exacerbated in recent years by boys' greater involvement with playing computer games and is perhaps in some measure linked to the fact that girls are now nationally out-performing boys at GCSE and that the gap is getting wider.

Some would argue that those television programmes and videos favoured by children often provide stereotyped and processed images which require little imaginative input or effort from the watcher, thus limiting the imaginative capability of the child. Others, particularly in the wake of the James Bulger murder case, where the viewing of a particular video was popularly – though probably wrongly – regarded as a factor influencing behaviour, see videos and computer games as potentially desensitizing and damaging in their effects. There is a concern that certain videos and games present a two-dimensional world in which the main object is for a muscle-bound super hero to beat an enemy – preferably to a pulp. In a fantasy world of casual violence, heads may be torn off and innards ripped out. Games such as *Mortal Kombat* and *Street Fighter* are highly popular with young adolescents and more recent games such as *Doom* have been issued with an '18' certificate. There is a fear too that the images of violence and horror associated with some videos and some computer games may be feeding back into the books themselves. Certainly concern is expressed over the violent nature of some children's reading and particularly at the popularity of horror stories with young readers. The dilemma of a parent or teacher who, having succeeded in persuading a young adolescent to read rather than play computer games or watch television, finding that the chosen reading, shared by a group of friends, is uncensored adult horror fiction of the Stephen King variety, is not unknown.

By contrast, many teachers and educators would still subscribe to Dr Johnson's view that:

> 'I would let [a boy] at first read any English book which happens to engage his attention; because you have done a great deal when you have brought a boy to have entertainment from a book. He'll get better books afterwards.'
>
> (Boswell, 1791)

They take the same position as the respected children's author and educator Aidan Chambers, who believes that wide, voracious and indiscriminate reading is the base soil from which discrimination and taste eventually grow. Peter Dickinson enlivened the debate a quarter of a century ago with his trenchant 'A defence of rubbish' (1970) celebrating the wide range of reading he and millions of children had undertaken without coming to any perceptible harm – and many teachers would agree with him. However, Dickinson commented that he was not, of course, advocating a total lack of control: 'I have no doubt in my own mind that there are certain sorts of reading which are deleterious and from which a child should be discouraged.'

As teachers of English, as those who choose and use books with our classes, as librarians and as parents, decisions about what our children read are inescapably ours and we need both to consider our position on the issues and to be as informed as possible about what is available and how self-chosen reading might be linked to our own work.

The belief that there is a link between reading and viewing is made explicit in surveys such as that carried out by Gallup for BBC Education and reported in the *Times Educational Supplement* (Coughlan, 1993) which found that only 10 per cent of 9–12-year-old children spend more time reading than watching television. The main reason given by 60 per cent of children for not reading more was that watching television and video had displaced books. Recent headlines give some indication of the focus of popular concerns. They include 'Time To Adjust Our Sets?' (Young, 1993) which quotes the view of Philip Dodds, editor of the BFI's *Sight and Sound* magazine that 'Video is the Penguin of the late 20th century'. He goes on to remark that 'The trouble is that television has become a new folk devil'. A *Times* article (Preston, 1993) announces the findings of a survey commissioned by the frozen food company, Birds Eye, under the headline 'Children Spurn Books for Computers' and laments the fact that 'less than a third of primary students read for pleasure, with computer heroes such as Sonic the Hedgehog and Super Mario replacing the Famous Five and Billy Bunter as childhood icons'. This same trend is noted in a more recent NOP survey commissioned by the Royal Mail and reported by Nicholas Tucker in *The Independent* newspaper (1994) under the headline 'Bye-bye Biggles, Hello Hedgehog,' from which it transpires that whilst 99 per cent of 11–14-year olds were familiar with Sonic the Hedgehog, only 46 per cent had heard of Biggles and 13 per cent of Orlando the Marmalade Cat. Hardly a surprising finding perhaps and, as Tucker suggests, part of the concern may be prompted by older adults' nostalgia for vanished figures of their own childhood who have not stood the test of time: 'who now remembers Harry Wharton, Tom Merry or those other once-celebrated characters circulating around the ample figure of [Billy] Bunter?' he asks.

The reference to Bunter is a reminder that many of the concerns expressed about video games and violence are not new. George Orwell, in his essay *Boys' Weeklies* (1939), remarked with mixed feelings the passing of the gentler world of the *Gem* and *Magnet* and the rise of the then modern papers such as the *Skipper* and *Hotspur* in which the reader is led to identify with 'some single all-powerful character who dominates everyone about him and whose usual method of solving any problem is a sock on the jaw' – a method favoured by the heroes of numerous computer games of the 1990s. In many cases the scenes of violence now, as then, are – to borrow Orwell's phrase – 'remarkably harmless and unconvincing'. What exercised Orwell more than these fairly tepid English papers were the imported 'Yank mags' in which 'you get real blood-lust, really gory descriptions of the all-in, jump-on-his-testicles style of fighting written in a jargon that has been perfected by people who brood endlessly on violence,' and magazines in which women were routinely objectified, degraded and even tortured. In the 1950s, there was widespread concern about the American 'horror comics'. In the 1970s, there were similar concerns over highly commercial and violent books such as Robert Allen's *Skinhead, Suedehead* and *Boot Boys*; and later, in the 1980s, over the great wave of adolescent fiction, such as Larry Bograd's *Bad Apple*, imported from the States. Such books were characterized by Benton and Fox (1985) as 'recipe fictions . . . offering blatant tastes to satisfy adolescent appetites – a kind of literary fast food'.

There are now, as in the past, a number of different, though often related strands to these various concerns. At its simplest, there is a fear that reading of fiction is being squeezed out by other, more immediately gratifying and perhaps less-demanding attractions; that it is, in effect, dying out for some children. Further, there is a concern that even if children are reading, they are not reading material which has been traditionally read by young people and therefore, the cultural heritage of children's literature is being lost or displaced. At another level, there is a fear that is at times akin to a moral panic – that the 'wholesome' reading of a real or imagined 'golden age' has been replaced by tales of violence and horror which mirror the world of video films and computer games. The picture is unclear and it would seem important to find out what children's reading and viewing habits are at the present time.

Finding out about reading and viewing in the nineties

The survey of children's reading interests published by Whitehead in 1977 as *Children and their Books* (Whitehead *et al.*, 1977) remains the single most comprehensive study of children's voluntary reading in the past 25 years though there have been various other, smaller scale surveys on children's attitudes to reading, notably those by the APU in 1982, 1983 and 1987 (Gorman *et al.*, 1982, 1983).

The media world of the child in the 1990s is vastly more complex than that of the child of the 1970s when Whitehead reported his findings and in this context it is important to note that the Whitehead survey was based on data gathered by questionnaire in March 1971 – a quarter of a century ago – in a secondary school world composed largely of grammar and secondary modern schools as well as comprehensives. Apart from there being entirely new technologies to attract young people – video tape and computer and video games are the two obvious examples – it seems there has also been a significant, and often related change in publishing and in reading habits. Most teachers are aware that many of the fiction titles read by those at school today bear little resemblance to those reported by Whitehead and that they often deal with experiences which would have been unavailable in print to Whitehead's readership. A good example is the recent success of the *Point Horror* series whose popularity, particularly with girls, has been noted by many teachers. Some school librarians rejoice in the fact that their students borrow these books as fast as they are replaced on the shelves: others feel strongly enough about them to ban them from their libraries altogether. Whatever the rights and wrongs of the situation, it seems likely that relatively few teachers have adequate knowledge of the content of the stories and of the fascination they hold for a large number of their students.

Similarly, although teachers know that the reading of magazines, particularly by boys, has changed they are less likely to be aware of the degree of change. For instance, it seems likely that whilst the time available for reading has shrunk as a result of the burgeoning interest in video games, magazines devoted to video games and the electronic inheritors of the popular *Dungeons and Dragons* fantasies of a decade or more ago, may form a substantial part of the reading that boys actually do. Outside this particular culture for the most part, teachers often have only a sketchy knowledge of, say, *White Dwarf*, a popular title with younger adolescent boys. Similarly, it is of course possible that there is a link between viewing and reading and that a number of young people read books as a direct result of seeing them dramatized on the screen. There is an increasingly symbiotic relationship between the media where marketing 'tie-ins' of various sorts are common.

Television was well established in British homes in 1971 but the spread of the television and of videotape recorders to children's own rooms is a comparatively recent phenomenon. The young have far more control over their viewing than formerly. Another new feature in homes generally and also in children's own rooms is the video games machine – the Sega, Super Nintendo, Atari or Amiga – which can engross as much if not more time than television. Whitehead examined only the amount of *time* spent watching television, choosing to ignore the actual programmes watched. However, it seems possible that if there is a consistency in the type and amount of viewing undertaken by young people at particular ages, that here is another significant aspect of their lives which should be placed alongside their choice of magazines, video games and videos as defining their cultural milieu.

Voluntary reading in the nineties

Research undertaken in 1994 with a cross-section of over 700 Year 8 students and nearly 400 from Year 10 is revealing, particularly with regard to students' voluntary reading. As in the Whitehead survey of 23 years earlier, students were asked to list their self-chosen reading during the course of a single month during term time.

In the past month, 86 per cent of the Year 8 girls but only 70 per cent of the Year 8 boys had read a book, with the Year 8 girls averaging 3.16 books per month and the boys 1.57 books per month. The comparable figures for the Whitehead survey were that 76.7 per cent of Year 8 girls had read a book in the past month and that 66.8 per cent of the boys had done so with girls and boys averaging 2.48 and 1.99 books per month, respectively. These girls, it would

Table 5.1   Most widely read books in Year 8, 1971 (after Whitehead *et al.*, *Children and their Books*, Macmillan, Schools Council, 1977)

Rank	Title	Author	Percentage of age group
1	*Little Women**	L.M. Alcott	3
2	*Black Beauty**	A. Sewell	2.6
3	*Treasure Island**	R.L. Stevenson	2.1
4	*The Lion, The Witch and the Wardrobe*	C.S. Lewis	1.3
5	*Jane Eyre**	C. Brontë	1.2
6	*Heidi*	J. Spyri	1.2
7	*Oliver Twist**	C. Dickens	1.2
8	*The Secret Seven*	E. Blyton	1.1
9	*The Silver Sword*	I. Seraillier	1
10	*Tom Sawyer**	M. Twain	1
11	*What Katy Did**	S. Coolidge	1
12	*Good Wives**	L.M. Alcott	1
13	*Kidnapped**	R.L. Stevenson	1
14	*Journey To the Centre of the Earth**	J. Verne	0.8
15	*Alice in Wonderland**	L. Carroll	0.7
16	*Little Men**	L.M. Alcott	0.7
17	*The Railway Children*	E. Nesbit	0.7
18	*What Katy Did Next**	S. Coolidge	0.7
19	*Great Expectations**	C. Dickens	0.6
20	*The Hobbit*	J.R.R. Tolkien	0.6
21	*The Naughtiest Girl in the School*	E. Blyton	0.6
22	*Robin Hood**		0.6
23	*Robinson Crusoe**	D. Defoe	0.6
24	*The Wind in the Willows**	K. Grahame	0.6

* Pre-twentieth century.

appear were reading somewhat more and boys slightly fewer books than in the earlier survey. That boys generally read fewer books than girls is well documented but there may be indications in these figures that the gap is widening.

What is very different from the earlier survey and may account in large measure for the widening gap, is the *nature* of the books chosen by these Year 8 students for their voluntary reading. Basing their figures on students' responses to a question asking what books they had read in the past month, Whitehead *et al.* listed the 24 'Most widely read books' in this age group in 1971. They remarked with some surprise the overwhelmingly nineteenth century flavour of a list so 'redolent of the past', attributing it in large measure to the limited range of titles then available in school libraries and, presumably, on shelves at home (Table 5.1). Even so, and granting that grammar schools formed a large part of that survey, it is a list which many have viewed with

Table 5.2   Most widely read books in Year 8, 1994

Rank	Title	Author	Percentage of age group
1	Forever	J. Blume	4.01
2	The BFG	R. Dahl	3.08
3	The Secret Diary of Adrian Mole	S. Townsend	3.08
4	The Hitch Hiker*	R.L. Stine	2.46
5	Beach House*	R.L. Stine	2.00
6	Trick or Treat*	R.T. Cusick	1.85
7	The Cemetery*	D.E. Athkins	1.85
8	Boy	R. Dahl	1.69
9	The Witches	R. Dahl	1.69
10	13 Tales of Horror*	T. Pines (ed.)	1.54
11	Deenie	J. Blume	1.54
12	Funhouse*	D. Hoh	1.54
13	Matilda	R. Dahl	1.54
14	Mother's Helper*	A. Bates	1.54
15	Charlie and The Chocolate Factory	R. Dahl	1.38
16	Red Dwarf (various titles)	Grant and Naylor	1.38
17	The Baby-sitter III*	R.L. Stine	1.38
18	The Growing Pains of Adrian Mole	S. Townsend	1.38
19	The Snowman*	R.L. Stine	1.38
20	April Fools*	R.T. Cusick	1.23
21	Baby Sitters Club (various titles)	A.M. Martin	1.23
22	Freeze-Tag*	C.B. Cooney	1.23
23	Going Solo	R. Dahl	1.23
24	It's Not The End Of The World	J. Blume	1.23
25	Jurassic Park	M. Crichton	1.23
26	The Accident*	D. Hoh	1.23
27	The Baby-sitter*	R.L. Stine	1.23
28	The Lifeguard*	R.T. Cusick	1.23
29	The Twits	R. Dahl	1.23
30	The Vampire's Promise*	C.B. Cooney	1.23
31	Famous Five (various)	E. Blyton	1.08
32	Mrs Doubtfire	A. Fine	1.08
33	Teacher's Pet*	R.T. Cusick	1.08
34	The Cheerleader*	C.B. Cooney	1.08
35	The Dead Game*	A. Bates	1.08
36	The Fever*	D. Hoh	1.08
37	Are You There God, It's Me Margaret	J. Blume	0.92
38	Camp Fear*	C. Ellis	0.92
39	Dream Date*	S. Smith	0.92
40	Last Dance	C.B. Cooney	0.92
41	Mort	T. Pratchett	0.92

Table 5.2   (cont.)

Rank	Title	Author	Percentage of age group
42	*My Secret Admirer**	C. Ellis	0.92
43	*Reaper Man*	T. Pratchett	0.92
44	*The Girlfriend**	R.L. Stine	0.92
45	*The Train**	D. Hoh	0.92
46	*Truckers*	T. Pratchett	0.92

* *Point Horror* titles.

some scepticism. One could speculate that there was formerly perhaps a greater desire to please on the part of respondents. If that was the case, it seems not to be so now. The corresponding list derived from the same question asked in 1994 is a marked contrast (Table 5.2).

It is not difficult to see why those who cherish a traditional view of what is appropriate reading for young people have been concerned. Not one of the Whitehead 'Top 24' titles appears in the first 46 of the 1994 list. There is no title drawn from the nineteenth century and indeed the most venerable is probably one of the Enid Blyton *Famous Five* titles (which by rights, if they were listed separately, would not make it into the Top 46 at all). The weightier 'classic' children's books of the period which often have an unequivocal social, moral or religious intent, and provided a demanding read have been displaced from the top of the list by more accessible texts.

They have not vanished altogether: *Black Beauty*, in 47th place on the list was read by five students in the period under review, representing 0.77 per cent as a percentage of the age group. *The Wind in The Willows* was still read by three students (0.46 per cent) as was *Treasure Island*. Two readers each (0.30 per cent) recorded *What Katy Did*, *The Hobbit* and *The Lion, The Witch and The Wardrobe*; and single readers (0.15 per cent) kept green the memories of *Little Women*, *Jane Eyre*, *Tom Sawyer*, *What Katy Did Next*, *Journey to the Centre of the Earth* and *Alice in Wonderland*.

Unlike the authors of the 1971 list, many of the names on the 1994 list would be unknown to most adults. Dahl, Blume and Townsend would probably register with a fair number but who are Stine, Cusick, Athkins, Hoh, and so on? The answer is that they are all from the imported American *Point Horror* series of about 50 titles, and growing, which are strongly marketed in this country by Scholastic and Hippo books. The impact of *Point Horror* books can be gauged from Figure 5.1 which ranks the most frequently read authors by the number of their books read in the Year 8 sample over the period of one month and which also provides a cumulative total for all the *Point Horror* titles. The appetite for (fairly mild) horror stories of this kind at this age appears to be insatiable and some school librarians have more requests for books of this

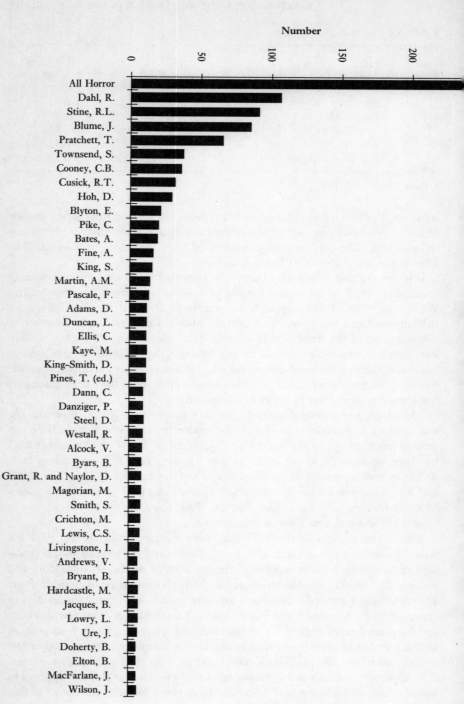

Figure 5.1 Authors most frequently read by Year 8 over a period of one month

type than any other. Some, however, will not purchase them, echoing the concern of those who feel that it is an inappropriate form of reading for schools to encourage. They are dismayed not just by the displacement of the classic children's texts (and here one would have to include the often quite demanding Puffin books of the 1960s and 1970s as well as the nineteenth century authors noted by Whitehead) but by what they see as the limited vocabulary, banal storylines and unhealthy preoccupations of the series. Significantly, many students purchase them for their own shelves and for circulation around a group of friends. Interestingly, although boys do read *Point Horror*, the main consumers are girls. The following comment written by a Year 8 girl is typical:

'I think the library needs more *Point Horror* books because friends of mine in Year 8 and Year 7 love the suspense and the sudden twist in the end. We all pass them round for each other to read.'

Another Year 8 girl, notes that four of the books she has read in the past month 'are from a series called *Point Horror*,' and continues:

'I have enjoyed all of these books and I am trying to read them all. *Point Horror* [books] can be very hard to get hold of because they are very popular.'

It is certainly the case that the greater amount of reading done by girls than boys is in some measure attributable to the popularity of this series which young adolescents find highly collectable: 'I am collecting all of the *Point Horror* [books] at the moment because I think they are really good books,' remarks one Year 8 girl. They are 'easy reads' – books that can be devoured at a sitting: 'I enjoy them very much because they're scary and I can get into them easily'; 'Quite scary but very easy and good to read' are typical comments. Peer group pressure is also clearly a significant factor in their continued success.

Writers such as Charles Sarland (1991) have commented more fully on the attractions of the adult horror fiction – for example, the novels of Virginia Andrews, Stephen King and James Herbert – to which many graduate at a later stage and which a number of the Year 8 students already enjoy. In the context of this chapter, suffice it to say that the roots of these simpler tales are often to be found in the urban legend as documented by scholars such as Brunvand (1983). The stories are frequently developments of those which have for many years circulated among school students and which have a wide, international currency; indeed some, like the babysitter tales, have provided the storylines of full-length horror films. To a certain extent, they appeal at this age because they are dealing at one remove and vicariously with some of the deepest fears of the child on the verge of adulthood – awakening sexuality, fear for one's personal safety in this context, personal identity, jealousy, family crisis and death.

The bones of traditional folk tales are often visible beneath the twentieth century surface slickness of these productions. It seems likely that in some degree they perform a similar service and offer a similar fascination to that offered by the older tales. It is worth reminding ourselves that many tales traditionally told to children draw on images no less horrific than anything modern writers produce. Severed limbs, a pickaxe through the skull, a heel chopped off and bleeding to fit in a shoe, red–hot iron shoes that sear into flesh causing the wearer to dance in agony, a wolf awaiting a young girl in her grand-mother's bed, a mermaid whose every step in human form is excruciating pain and like treading on sharp knives and who has her tongue cut out – these are the currency not even of adolescent reading but of the stories we readily tell to quite young children.

It is instructive to compare both the treatment and the language of the story of Mr Fox, a nineteenth century version of which is collected by Angela Carter in *The Virago Book of Fairy Tales* (1992) with the modern *Point Horror* story. Mr Fox, who has an appetite for dragging young maidens to his Bloody Chamber where he murders them, is betrothed to Lady Mary. She, being a woman of independent spirit, hides herself away in Mr Fox's house where she witnesses his dark deeds:

> Just as he got near Lady Mary, Mr Fox saw a diamond ring glittering on the finger of the young lady he was dragging, and he tried to pull it off. But it was tightly fixed and would not come off, so Mr Fox cursed and swore, and drew his sword, raised it and brought it down on the hand of the poor young lady. The sword cut off the hand, which jumped up into the air, and fell of all places in to Lady Mary's lap . . .

The denouement of the story, where Lady Mary accuses Mr Fox of his crimes, is equally robust:

> 'It is not so, nor it was not so. And God forbid it should be so,' said Mr Fox, and was going to say something else as he rose from his seat, when Lady Mary cried out:
> 'But it is so, and it was so. Here's hand and ring I have to show,' and pulled out the lady's hand from her dress, and pointed it straight at Mr Fox.
> At once her brothers and her friends drew their swords and cut Mr Fox into a thousand pieces.

Point Horror books also offer storylines moved along by action delineated in very simple language, with short sentences and stereotyped images. Like the ballads, and like many folk tales, but rather more crudely, they tell of bloody murders, revenants, of vengeful spirits, of lost loves, of the dead beginning to speak. Violence is common and – a major difference from the traditional tale – it is sometimes lovingly detailed as though on film.

In Christopher Pike's *Collect Call Part II*, one of the stories in the popular *13 Tales of Horror* (1991) as elsewhere in *Point Horror*, there is much in the way of helplessness in the face of evil – often involving cruel bonds cutting into female flesh. Dragged by her hair, dazed and as 'blood seeped down the back of her neck, soaking her blouse', Caroline is thrown against the 'gnarled trunk' of a tree by a teenage psychopathic killer whose hobby it is to bury girls alive in the local graveyard. Mr Fox, in one of his many guises, is alive and well and living in the United States:

> From his pocket he drew forth a thin length of rope. Her arms were yanked behind her back. Another wave of pain shot through her body . . . Bobby paused in his knot, trying to press his mouth against her cheek. His teeth scratched her soft flesh. 'You don't know how close we are, babe.'

After much straining against the cords, Caroline does escape burial in her friend's coffin. Bobby tells her,

> 'I don't want to hurt you too bad before I put you inside. I like to hear a girl kick before the mud settles on top of her.'

The tables are turned and (a moral ending, perhaps?), Caroline

> belted him in the face with the shovel . . . a fat line of blood split his expression in two and he went down. She raised the shovel again and brought it down hard on the back of his skull.

Caroline is as feisty a young woman as Lady Mary but instead of an almost stylized and distanced situation, we are presented with a realistically detailed representation.

In *The Hitchhiker* by R.L. Stine (1993), a two-page description of a young man being eaten alive by piranha fish reads in part:

> Art resurfaced one more time.
> One arm reached for the sky.
> The other hung lifelessly in the red water.
> Chunks of flesh had been eaten away. Art floated in a circle of dark blood. His head bobbed on the surface like a wooden buoy, cut and bleeding.
> James saw the deep gash at Art's throat. Saw bone exposed at Art's shoulder. Saw the fleshless legs float to the top, no longer kicking.

It does not improve. There is evidence from students' comments that some do begin to grow out of such tales. The twist in the tail of the *Point Horror* story comes to be expected and as such is predictable, comforting and, ultimately, for some readers, boring. Evidence from the Year 10 survey suggests that *Point Horror* is still a staple for many students at that age and still accounted for around a quarter of all the fiction read by the Year 10. Horror stories generally were easily the largest single category read by this age group: growing out of early adolescent horror can mean growing into its adult counterpart.

Reading *Point Horror* is in some measure, perhaps, proof to others and to oneself of having arrived at a certain stage in development. In a similar way perhaps, but on a much more limited scale, many adolescent readers in the 1950s and 1960s challenged themselves with adult narratives by Dennis Wheatley. *Point Horror* stories might also be seen as constituting a rite of passage, a proof of a certain kind of 'maturity' and of toughness. They form an underground of stories in a very similar way to that of the urban legend, but in this case not passed orally in whispered conversations but physically from hand to hand as relatively cheap mass-produced texts. In this context, it is worth observing that books are increasingly sold through smoothly organized, highly computerized operations such as those of W.H. Smith and school book clubs: what sells is what appears on the shelves and gets publicized.

The adolescent readership is targeted as never before. Does this mean that the adolescent readership is exploited as never before? If one applies the checklist suggested by Benton and Fox (1985): Are the writers pandering to the adolescent inclination to self-absorption? Are they nihilistic? Are their stories clichéd in terms of plot and character? Is there a real possibility that the books will expand or open up some area of understanding concerning character, place or social, moral and political circumstances? Are the adults in the stories two dimensional and incapable of growth? Is the dialogue synthetic? – then one must question whether many, if any, of these books offer genuine possibilities of 'growing up through stories'.

Charles Sarland (1995) sees the engagement with horror in a positive light. Normal, healthy 12-year olds have no difficulty in distinguishing fiction from reality, he asserts and they are 'perfectly capable of saying "no" to horror if they think it is going to be too frightening for them'. Horror 'strengthens the emotional muscles', defines cultural limits for the young and makes clear what is forbidden by society 'without preaching and with a vividness and clarity that is not available elsewhere.'

Sarland suggests that good teachers know that the implication that it is not possible to good work with classes with popular material such as *Point Horror* books is nonsense. Experience would suggest that he has a point. He cites a teacher involving her Year 9 class with activities 'ranging from more formal analysis of character, plot and narrative perspective, to the more creative activities – writing blurbs and advertising copy, constructing alternative endings, writing play synopses, preparing film scripts, designing book covers, etc. that are the stock in trade of the good English classroom'. The students' work was 'vibrant and alive' and Sarland makes the point that the teacher was only able to develop this work because the boycott of Key Stage 3 SATs at the time gave her the space to capitalize on the students' enthusiasms. Given texts that speak so strongly to adolescents' interests, it would seem absurd to ignore them; good sense to find ways of incorporating them into our teaching and unwise to condemn them with that righteousness so often reserved for what others we would wish to control, choose to do. However, the teacher's stance is one that needs careful consideration.

It is difficult to know whether the success of these titles will be short-lived, a fashionable trend to be overtaken by something else in a year or two but, given the deep roots of many of these stories and the way in which they are tailored to fill certain needs and then skilfully marketed, it seems likely that they and their successors will be around for some years and that teachers need to consider their response to them, weighing up the benefits against their concerns. For many teachers, the bottom line is that they are pleased when students who have been reluctant readers become hooked on these stories. At least they are reading and enjoying it. And reading leads on to more reading, 'the reading habit'. The question then arises as to whether the habit is the habit of reading stories of ever-increasing horror or perhaps the habit of reading only books within the series rather than reading more widely. Good teachers can undoubtedly use these books to provide a stepping stone to something more substantial (one thinks of the teacher who made a valuable connection between *Point Horror* and Robert Westall for several students): and to do that, they need to have some acquaintance with what fascinates their students so much.

The pattern of reading in the Year 10 sample is in many ways similar to that of those in Year 8 and follows the same downward trend in boys' reading noted by Whitehead. In 1971, 40 per cent of the boys and 32.4 per cent of the girls had read no books of their own choice during the preceding month: in 1994, 53.5 per cent of boys and 36.4 per cent of girls recorded no books read of their own choice in the previous month. Again, with two notable exceptions, the *nature* of the books read in 1994 was largely different from that of the Whitehead survey. Remarkably, the 1971 list was headed by *Little Women*, and followed by the violent *Skinhead* each read by 1.7 per cent of the age group. Perhaps this was the first intimation of the pattern of reading that was to develop over the next quarter of a century. *Day of the Triffids, Jane Eyre, Animal Farm, Oliver Twist* and *Lord of the Flies* were next in order, reasserting the traditional 'quality' reading list. *Love Story* followed equalling the popularity of *Nineteen Eighty Four* and then came *Where Eagles Dare, The Chrysalids, Cider with Rosie* and *Treasure Island*. *Hell's Angels*, celebrating the bike boys as *Skinhead* had celebrated the boot boys, followed before the classic titles resumed with *War of the Worlds, Black Beauty* and *Wuthering Heights*. The 1994 Year 10 list is, as one might expect, very different though, as in 1971, past and present mingle on more equal terms (Table 5.3).

Point Horror titles account for 24 per cent of all books read by Year 10 students during the month in question and, if the adult horror titles are added, then something approaching a third of the books could be said to have a horror element. Nonetheless, Judy Blume retains her pre-eminence as most read author and there is a strong representation from comic Science fiction fantasy writers such as Grant and Naylor and Douglas Adams. A handful of titles appeared on the 1971 list, most notably *Jane Eyre, Cider with Rosie* and *Lord of the Flies*. Film tie-ins are more common with the older age group's choices. The popularity of the *Red Dwarf* books is solely attributable to their being first a television series; *Jurassic Park* and *Robin Hood* had been hugely promoted as films in preceding months; *The Shining* was available on video and *Schindler's List* (the film) and *Schindler's Ark* (the book) were enjoying huge critical acclaim. Often popular adult writers are those with something of a blockbuster

Table 5.3   Most widely read books in Year 10, 1994

Rank	Title	Author	Percentage of age group
1	Forever	J. Blume	1.8
2	Red Dwarf (various)	Grant and Naylor	1.5
3	The Baby-sitter*	R.L. Stine	1.5
4	Trick or Treat*	R.T. Cusick	1.5
5	Flowers in the Attic	V. Andrews	1.3
6	Hitch-hikers' Guide to the Galaxy	D. Adams	1.3
7	IT	S. King	1.3
8	Jane Eyre	C. Brontë	1.3
9	Jurassic Park	I. Crichton	1.3
10	Life, The Universe and Everything	D. Adams	1.3
11	The Beach House*	R.L. Stine	1.3
12	The Boyfriend*	R.L. Stine	1.3
13	The Girlfriend*	R.L. Stine	1.3
14	The Shining	S. King	1.3
15	To Kill a Mockingbird	H. Lee	1.3
16	Goodnight Mr Tom	M. Magorian	1.0
17	Misery	S. King	1.0
18	Mostly Harmless	D. Adams	1.0
19	Needful Things	S. King	1.0
20	Pet Sematary	S. King	1.0
21	Restaurant at the End of the Universe	D. Adams	1.0
22	Robin Hood (Prince of Thieves)	S. Green	1.0
23	Roll of Thunder Hear My Cry	M.D. Taylor	1.0
24	Schindler's List	T. Keneally	1.0
25	Sharpe (various stories)	B. Cornwell	1.0
26	Teacher's Pet*	R.T. Cusick	1.0
27	The Firm	J. Grisham	1.0
28	The Train*	D. Hoh	1.0
29	A Summer to Die	L. Lowry	0.8
30	April Fools*	R.T. Cusick	0.8
31	Bravo Two Zero	A. McNab	0.8
32	Brighton Rock	G. Greene	0.8
33	Cider With Rosie	L. Lee	0.8
34	Deenie	J. Blume	0.8
35	Dragon Tears	D.R. Koontz	0.8
36	Goggle Eyes	A. Fine	0.8
37	Lord of the Flies	W. Golding	0.8
38	Matilda	R. Dahl	0.8
39	Philadelphia	C. Davies	0.8
40	Polo	J. Cooper	0.8
41	Redwall	B. Jacques	0.8
42	Tess of the d'Urbervilles	T. Hardy	0.8
43	Beach Party*	R.L. Stine	0.8

Table 5.3 (cont.)

Rank	Title	Author	Percentage of age group
44	The Cemetery*	D.E. Athkins	0.8
45	The Hobbit	J.R.R. Tolkien	0.8
46	The Liar	F. Fry	0.8
47	The Lifeguard*	R.T. Cusick	0.8
48	The Rats	J. Herbert	0.8
49	The Snowman*	R.L. Stine	0.8
50	The Waitress*	S. Smith	0.8

* *Point Horror* titles.

reputation in their fields: Stephen King, John Grisham and Jilly Cooper, for example. If one counts the number of mentions made of single authors, rather than individual books, then R.L. Stine and Stephen King easily top the list with Judy Blume and Douglas Adams coming third and fourth, respectively. Christopher Pike, Virginia Andrews, R.T. Cusick and Dean R. Koontz are next in order. All four are American and all four are specialists in horror.

For those to whom reading is inescapably bound up with the promulgation of a national cultural identity, the 1994 lists provide further problems. It is very largely the *American* horror novel that dominates, though individually, Judy Blume described by John Rowe Townsend as 'the great communicator with adolescents' (Townsend, 1990) takes the crown in Year 8 with her highly popular stories focusing on aspects of growing up. Significantly, a fair number of the British writers who are enjoyed by children of this age are a healthily irreverent bunch – Sue Townsend, Roald Dahl, Grant and Naylor (authors of the *Red Dwarf* television series) and Terry Pratchett in Year 8; Grant and Naylor, and Douglas Adams in Year 10. Perhaps it is in part a response, conscious or otherwise, to such changes which prompts the strong and oft-repeated insistence of those who frame the National Curriculum upon 'our culture' and 'cultural heritage' and reinforces the requirement that pre-twentieth century literature should be studied. By choice, most of these students' favourite reading is not predominantly of English or British authors; and even where modern native writers flourish they habitually and almost without exception are cynical about or cock a snook at authority.

For those who are exercised over the cultural heritage model of English and reading there is a clear erosion of all that they hold dear. It seems probable that there is a massive cultural change under way which can only accelerate over the coming years, particularly as convergence in the media becomes more pronounced. The likelihood must be that the traditional canon of children's literature in English will continue to fade, though individual stories may be given the kiss of life through television serialization. The cultural capital that such stories represent and the images of virtue, of manly or womanly behaviour they provide will be less and less accessible – an outcome that provokes feelings either of satisfaction or of dismay according to where one stands. Perhaps more worrying is the way in which the new classics of the past thirty years (often described as 'a golden age of children's literature') also appear to be fading for the younger age group. Presented with the findings of the 1994 survey recently, a number of teachers remarked that they felt they were under such pressure to present Shakespeare and pre-twentieth century literature that they had not sufficient time to introduce their classes to many of the modern classics which had hitherto formed a major part of their teaching.

The Whitehead survey felt able to divide the books read by children into 'quality' and 'non-quality' narrative. Behind that apparently simple distinction are a host of essentially Leavisite assumptions about the texts which it would be inappropriate to examine in depth here. It seems likely, however, that very few of the most frequently read texts of the 1994 list would have been given the seal of quality by the Whitehead team, though most of the 1971 list merits their approval. Of the Year 8 reading, one guesses that Dahl's autobiographical *Boy* would be acceptable but beyond that, one cannot be sure that any title in the recent list would make it. A pity, surely, for a young reader who has taken aboard even a fraction of the complex intertextual humour and social comment of a Terry Pratchett novel is reading at a very high level indeed. As Marina Warner (1994) remarks:

> Today, writers for children (and sometimes for adults, too) who draw on fairytale motifs and characters, like (*inter alia*) Terry Pratchett, are conjuring up dream worlds as personally idealistic, as politically socially contentious, and often as spiritually wary and iconoclastic, as their more apparently sophisticated precursors, Erasmus, Voltaire and Swift.

Rather more, but still a minority, of the most popular Year 10 books would fall into the old 'quality' category. The 'quality/non-quality' distinction is too simplistic: on the other hand, it must be acknowledged that it would be difficult to defend much of the self-chosen reading on grounds of merit.

However, the Year 8 group named 929 separate titles that they had read in the past month and it is important not to be misled by the 'Top 46' list into thinking all of their reading is of a piece. We should recognize the remarkable range of the reading undertaken. Many of the nineteenth century works are still there, albeit in smaller numbers – in addition to the ones listed earlier, *Tom Brown's Schooldays*, *Dr Jekyll and Mr Hyde*, *Jane Eyre* and *Tess of the d'Urbervilles* are all represented. Of twentieth century titles, the range is enormous – everything from *The Color Purple* to *The Secret Diary of John Major*.

A similar range of reading is discernible in Year 10 where small numbers of students read books as diverse as *A Pair of Blue Eyes*, *A Room with a View*, *Brave New World*, *Candide*, *The French Lieutenant's Woman*, *Gaelic is Fun*, *The Great British Pub Guide*, *Great Expectations*, *Greek Myths*, *How to Excite Your*

Man in Bed, The Kama Sutra, Love in a Time of Cholera, Nazi Regalia, Oranges Are Not The Only Fruit, Pilgrim's Progress, SAS Survival Handbook, Sons and Lovers and *Zen and the Art of Motor-cycle Maintenance*. Quite what advice one might offer to the student who recorded his month's reading as consisting of *The Encyclopaedia of Forensic Science, Great Crimes and Trials of the Twentieth Century, The Murder Guide, Murderous Women, The Afterlife,* and *The Name of the Beast,* is unclear. He had, as he quite reasonably explained, joined a Crime book club and these things interested him.

One discernible trend which does not show up in the 1994 'Top 46' list for Year 8 and could not have appeared in the 1971 list, is the interest in books which are aimed at the young adolescent's uncertainties about growing up and which contain advice on personal, health and sexual matters. There are a number of titles which individually just fail to qualify for the 'most widely read' list but collectively would do so. Among these are *Diary of A Teenage Health Freak; I'm a Teenage Health Freak Too; Coping With Boys* and *Coping with Girls.* Added together with one or two others with single mentions, this group of books would edge into fourth place in the 1994 list and they clearly perform a valuable service. According to one Year 8 girl,

> *Coping with Boys* is a very good book. It says what you should do if a boy is horrible to you. I would give it 10 out of 10.

A major part of the appeal of Judy Blume's books is, of course, that they provide similar advice in the more accessible fictional form. The appeal of the lugubrious Adrian Mole is not unconnected with this desire to tease out teenage problems. By Year 10 such titles, apart from the Judy Blume and Adrian Mole books have all but disappeared from the lists.

Students were asked if they had a favourite author. As in the earlier survey, this question was answered by something more than half the Year 8 respondents. The request for 'a favourite author' was often ignored, so keen were some to list two or even three favourites. As a result, one must treat the figures with some caution. Nonetheless, it comes as no surprise to find Roald Dahl topping the list with a runaway 122 mentions and Judy Blume coming second with 48. Terry Pratchett just beats into fourth place Enid Blyton who in turn is just ahead of two modern horror writers, R.L. Stine and Stephen King with 20 and 16, respectively. This last is a surprise, perhaps, because none of his titles features in the Top 46 most widely read books: in fact, he has a steady readership of *a range* of his books by a number of students. Other horror writers in the top dozen named here would include R.T. Cusick at number 8, undifferentiated *Point Horror* at number 10 and Christopher Pike, at number 11. Whatever one feels about the nature of the changes, there will undoubtedly be those who, amazed at her staying power, are nonetheless delighted to see Enid Blyton tumbled from the remarkable eminence she held in 1971 where, over three year groups, she recorded more than 10 times the number of mentions as favourite writer than the next challenger – Charles Dickens – about whose appearance so high on the list, the Whitehead team were somewhat sceptical.

It does not appear on this evidence that there has been a great falling off in the reading of fiction in the earlier years of secondary school but that markedly less is read by choice at the Year 10 stage. The nature of that reading has changed substantially. It is more worldly-wise, it is more 'adult' in certain ways and it is more concerned with the individual and his or (more usually) her personal problems. The demands of a *Point Horror* are not great but then neither were the demands of the then ubiquitous Enid Blyton. Most of the horror stories are relatively tame, though one might have a legitimate concern about the way in which they seem to take over some children's reading so completely. The literature beloved by former generations is still there but is a fading presence. In Year 8 there is a refreshing desire to use books for finding out about oneself and human relationships and some would find the popularity of books that are questioning and irreverent in their attitudes to social convention equally refreshing. One cannot know, but it seems at least possible that today's youngsters are more honest in their responses and less trammelled by what convention expected of them: although they follow fashions, many individuals appear to be remarkably independent readers. In Year 10, particularly, the range of books read was wide and the content often very challenging: a number of students were taking on the most demanding of adult texts. That said, what must be a cause for concern is the 30 per cent of boys in Year 8 and the 53 per cent of boys in Year 10 who claimed to have read no books of their own choosing in the previous month. The importance of the teacher and of the librarian cannot be stressed too much in helping to change these figures.

Other reading: magazines and periodicals

The Whitehead team of the 1970s felt able to state unequivocally that 'comics are the most potent form of periodical reading for the majority of the age range we are concerned with' (Whitehead *et al.*, 1977). The 'Top 10' periodicals read by each of the Year 8 age group in 1971 and 1994 are listed in Tables 5.4 and 5.5, respectively.

If the 1994 list is extended to take account of the multitudinous periodicals read by this age group, the pattern remains constant. Boys read a huge range of non-fiction magazines concerned with computers and video games or with sport (notably football, angling and cars/motor bikes/mountain bikes). Many of these titles are also bought and read by adult males. Apart from a few mentions of football magazines, girls read very little in any of these areas preferring (or being conditioned towards?) periodicals concerned with the pop scene and fashion, romance, personal problems and television soaps. Some, but one would hazard relatively few, of these titles are bought and read by adult females. In both boys' and girls' periodicals, there is a tendency, except in some of the computer magazines, to more and bigger pictures and less and less text.

Table 5.4 'Top 10' periodicals read by Year 8 students in 1971

Boys	Percentage	Girls	Percentage
Beano	27.0	Bunty	28.9
Dandy	24.4	Jackie	25.7
Shoot	17.3	Mandy	21.0
Victor	15.3	Judy	18.5
Goal	13.0	Beano	17.2
Tiger	12.3	Dandy	15.1
Beezer	11.3	Diana	12.2
Scorcher	10.6	June	10.1
Topper	10.4	Tammy	9.6
Lion & Thunder	8.7	Romeo	9.2

Table 5.5 'Top 10' periodicals read by Year 8 students in 1994

Boys	Percentage	Girls	Percentage
Match	20.0	Just 17	62.8
Shoot	17.5	Big!	50.0
Beano	12.7	Smash Hits	42.4
Dandy	7.0	Shout	29.0
90 Minutes	6.3	Mizz	24.2
Gamesmaster	5.7	Fast Forward	18.8
Mean machines	5.4	TV Hits	11.6
Nintendo Magazine	5.0	More	8.0
Sega Power	5.0	Horse & Pony	5.9
White Dwarf	4.4	Live & Kicking	5.6

A similar division is apparent in the lists for Year 10 which in 1971 were topped by *Shoot, Goal* and *Beano* for the boys and by *Jackie* (58.0 per cent), *Loving* and *Mirabelle* for the girls. In 1994, *Just 17, Mizz, Smash Hits, Big* and *More* headed the lists for girls: various *Amiga* and *Sega* computer games magazines, *Shoot, Match* and various car magazines were those most read by boys. The reading demands of most of these comics and magazines are very simple, though some of the more technical magazines present fairly complex specialized vocabulary.

The importance of periodical reading either in terms of modifying individuals' sensibility or as a means of encouraging the reading habit is impossible to quantify. Much of it can be taken in with an eye to the pictures and little concern for the words, and much of it serves to underline and confirm the most basic gender stereotypes. However, compared with the adolescent world of 1971, that of 1994 is much more 'adult' in so many ways – particularly for the female readership. Gone are the relatively childish *Bunty*, *Mandy* and *Judy*: even the rather more sophisticated *Jackie* has ceased publication. In their place are magazines designed to appeal to and to flatter a much more independent, aspirational and worldly-wise adolescent. It is no accident that the title most read by 12–13-year olds is *Just 17*.

The girls' teen magazines are much more carefully targeted at their audience, much more conscious of, and outspoken about matters such as sexual relations and drugs both in their story lines and their advice columns; inevitably, and probably rightly, raising awareness of areas such as AIDS, contraception and sexual abuse as well as peddling much of the same formula romance and pop entertainment of the past. In many cases, there is fairly dense and demanding prose, particularly in some of the advice columns, and it cannot simply be dismissed as easy reading. It is also very clear that girls in particular feel they now have to read one or more of the leading magazines to be both informed about a range of serious concerns and to be in the swim in terms of current trends in music and fashion.

The boys' chosen reading never touches on these matters. Girls, it is assumed, will be more interested in and responsive to the human interest angle, to personal relationships: boys, it is assumed, will be more interested in *things*, in competitive sport, in control and power and in the technical. Boys have stayed remarkably faithful to the kind of comic or magazine they read in 1971 with several titles staying the same. Their top five still include three football publications and two traditional comics. Computer and video-games magazines account for a far higher proportion of the boys' reading than might appear from the list. There are scores of individual and specialist titles catering for a variety of computers and games systems. Many boys are also deeply into fantasy war-gaming, served by certain specialist magazines, which is also to do with exercising control, power, gaining advantage and mastering masses of technical minutiae. The one allowable concession to the foibles of human nature is in the immature humour of the traditional comic, *Dandy* or *Beano* – both still occupying their timewarp – for the many; *Viz* (which comes in at number 11 and delights in the 'arrested development' school of male humour with its obsessive emphasis on bodily functions) is for the sophisticates. The extent to which these markedly different styles of publication reflect or cause gender stereotyping and attitudes cannot be addressed here: there can be little doubt that they reinforce them and that such views and attitudes are often reflected in the opinions voiced by students in discussion and writing as well as in the storylines they develop in their own work (see both Gemma Moss, 1989, and Charles Sarland, 1995, for a fuller discussion of this).

Television viewing

It comes as no surprise to learn that over 99 per cent of the students in Years 8 and 10 had a television in their own home. Perhaps more startlingly, 70 per

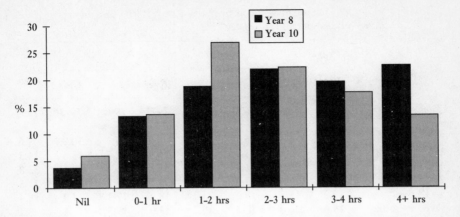

Figure 5.2   Hours of television watched by Years 8 and 10 the previous day

cent of Year 8 and Year 10 students had a television in their own room. Over 27 per cent of Year 8 students and 28.6 per cent of Year 10 students also had a video cassette player in their own room. Slightly less than half of Year 8 (46 per cent) had a video games machine in the home and slightly more than half (51 per cent) had a video games machine in their room. The figures for Year 10 were slightly lower – 42 per cent in each case.

Clearly, one major change since the Whitehead survey is the accessibility of television and the degree of independent control that most young people can exercise over their viewing. The implications for reading, simply in terms of the time available for books, are likely to be important. Figure 5.2, showing the percentage watching television on the previous weekday, makes it clear that very few watched no television and that in Year 8, nearly 23 per cent watched more than 4 hours in the course of the day. The figures are remarkably similar to those of the Whitehead survey but the type of programme favoured by the young viewer has undoubtedly changed. It should also be noted that in addition to watching broadcast programmes, many watched videos for a substantial length of time.

A tabular version of Figure 5.2 (see Table 5.6) indicates how these hours are shared between boys and girls in each year group and compares the 1994 figures with those established by Whitehead in 1971. There is a strong similarity between the figures for 1971 and 1994 and in both surveys the pattern for Years 8 and 10 is generally very consistent. The 26 per cent of Year 8 boys watching more than 4 hours of television on weekdays is perhaps unexpected. Given these figures, it is hardly surprising that nearly 72 per cent of boys and 52 per cent of girls in the Year 8 sample agreed with the proposition 'I prefer watching television to reading books'. The equivalent figures for Year 10 are 75 per cent of boys and 48 per cent of girls.

In view of the expressed preferences for magazine reading, it is equally

Table 5.6   Hours of television watched by Years 8 and 10 the previous day: boys versus girls: 1971 versus 1994

| | Year 8 | | | | Year 10 | | | |
| | Boys (%) | | Girls (%) | | Boys (%) | | Girls (%) | |
Time	1971	1994	1971	1994	1971	1994	1971	1994
Nil	5.6	3.1	5.2	4.0	8.0	7.1	10.9	4.6
Under 1 hour	9.4	13.6	11.2	13.3	14.4	12.7	15.6	14.3
1–2 hours	23.9	20.3	21.1	17.3	21.3	20.4	22.6	32.8
2–3 hours	23.3	20.9	23.9	22.6	23.1	23.2	21.6	21.5
3–4 hours	18.2	15.8	18.2	23.2	18.2	17.1	14.9	18.4
Over 4 hours	19.6	26.0	20.3	19.5	15.0	19.3	14.4	8.2

unsurprising that the types of television programme watched are predominantly the soaps. Asked which programmes they 'always try to watch,' the imported Australian soaps *Neighbours* and *Home and Away* easily topped the Year 8 list with 59.4 per cent and 48.9 per cent, respectively. The home-grown *Eastenders* took third place with 30.2 per cent. Just over 19 per cent of Year 8 students 'always try to watch' the comedy sci-fi space drama, *Red Dwarf*. The police drama *The Bill* was watched regularly by 14.9 per cent and 12 per cent watched 999.

Favourite programmes in Year 10 followed a virtually identical pattern and similar percentages with *Neighbours, Home and Away* and *Eastenders* in the first three positions and *The Bill* and *Red Dwarf* in fourth and fifth places. There is a remarkable similarity both in time spent and in programmes watched across the two age groups, perhaps indicative of a much more homogeneous teenage culture than formerly, extending perhaps from around 11–12 years of age to 15–16 years.

In both year groups, the types of programme watched are in marked contrast with those noted in a survey published in 1973 for the Schools Council (Murdock and Phelps, 1973). This survey listed the types of television programmes most frequently mentioned as favourites by interviewees (Table 5.7).

The appeal of the Australian soaps is largely that they deal with family issues and focus very much on the various entanglements, amorous and otherwise, of the attractive younger characters. Like the teen magazines they focus on relationships and they frequently offer moral and social dilemmas to be resolved. English teachers have often remarked on the way that the Romeo and Juliet situation of star-crossed lovers from rival families is recycled from time to time in *Neighbours*. The soaps also offer fantasy role models and many of the characters have lifestyles and relationships that appeal greatly to a sizeable group of young British teenagers. Again, for those who feel that the cultural

Table 5.7 Most popular TV shows in 1973 (after Murdock and Phelps, *Mass Media in the Secondary School*, 1973)

Type of programme	Second-year students (Year 8), n = 67	Fourth-year students (Year 10), n = 167
Comedy	24	18
Children's	21	4
Investigation	13	12
Science fiction	11	10
Pop music	10	24

milieu of the young is formed as much by what they choose to watch as by what they read and who feel strongly about where the national culture should be located, there must be some cause for concern here. The old empire has struck back, and Australian soaps hold our young viewers in thrall as surely as American authors command the bulk of their popular reading.

In this, of course, they are not greatly different from their parents. As Mark Lawson remarks:

> . . . the bi-weekly, tri-weekly or daily serial has become the most powerful narrative form ever devised. No book, no newspaper and almost no film is consumed by 18 million Britons, and still less by that number every few days for decades.
> (Lawson, 1995)

As a powerful literary form capable, unlike other forms of fiction, of unfolding a life in real time and, at their best, 'creating a richness of relationship between the character and viewer' (Lawson), the soaps are worth our serious study. *Neighbours* and *Home and Away* are dramatically not in the same league as the British soaps which are watched much more by adults, but they do provide a stepping stone. In common with these older soaps they also offer what Lawson remarks as the second unusual distinction of soap as a fictional form: that nearly all of its famous characters have been women. The original aim in having so many female roles was to appeal to the captive 'housewife' audience of long ago, but 'writers and actresses subverted this by creating some of the strongest and most interesting women in fiction'. The appeal of the soap to teenage girls in particular is hardly surprising.

The watching of videos formed a comparatively small but significant *addition* to the watching of broadcast television during the week already noted. Fourteen per cent of Year 8 boys and 10 per cent of girls watched videos for up to an hour on the previous day; nearly 17 per cent of boys and 13 per cent of girls watched videos for 1–2 hours; 11.4 per cent of boys watched them for 2–3 hours but only 3.7 per cent of girls. Nearly 3 per cent of the Year 8 boys clocked up over 4 hours of video viewing on the preceding weekday evening. Figures for the Year 10 sample indicate that slightly less time was spent in

Table 5.8   Time spent playing computer games 1994*

Time	Year 8		Year 10	
	Boys (%)	Girls (%)	Boys (%)	Girls (%)
Nil	37.8	74.9	48.6	82.2
Under 1 hour	26.4	14.2	21.5	11.6
1–2 hours	19.1	8.3	14.9	4.5
2–3 hours	7.3	2.4	8.8	1.0
3–4 hours	4.4	–	3.3	0.5
Over 4 hours	4.7	–	2.7	–

* In addition to time spent watching television and videos.

video viewing by both boys and girls with, for example, about 13 per cent of boys and 7.6 per cent of girls watching videos for 1–2 hours. What is perhaps most important to note is that 46.8 per cent of boys and 28.8 per cent of girls in Year 8 and 36 per cent of boys and 23 per cent of girls in Year 10 watched a video for some space of time on the preceding weekday.

It is not all bad news for those concerned about reading: a small number of each sample reported that they had read stories because they had either seen the film, television serialization or the video first. Among these, for example, would be Michael Crichton's *Jurassic Park* which was mentioned by 29 Year 8 students; *Mrs Doubtfire* and *Goggle Eyes*, both by Anne Fine, and various *Red Dwarf* and *Home Alone* spin-off publications were all mentioned by 7–14 students. Interestingly, a small number of Year 8 students also mentioned reading *The Silence of the Lambs, IT, Indecent Proposal* and *Sleeping With The Enemy* as a result of seeing them first on the screen.

Of course, broadcast programmes and videos are not the only lure offered by the domestic television screen: an increasing number of video games are being bought and played on consoles at home. Here again, the difference between boys' and girls' involvement with the medium is significant (Table 5.8).

Again, it is perhaps important to remember that these hourages are *in addition* to those already recorded as being spent watching television and videos. Of course, the same people do not necessarily undertake all three activities in the course of a day – though some do – but a large number of young people, particularly boys in Year 8, spend substantial amounts of time in front of a screen on weekdays watching television programmes, watching videos and playing computer games. Far more male respondents in both Years 8 and 10 were able to name a favourite computer game than could name a favourite author. Whereas 18.5 per cent of boys had more than 50 computer games at home, only 3.7 per cent of girls claimed to have that number. Sixty-nine per cent of boys and 32.6 per cent of girls in Year 8 agreed with the proposition that 'I prefer playing computer games to reading books'. The comparable figures for Year 10 are 69.7 per cent of boys but only 20 per cent of girls.

It would be easy, to ascribe boys' lack of interest in reading to long hours spent watching television and playing computer games but the evidence is not so clear-cut. Undoubtedly it is true of a substantial number of non-reading boys that they spend their time in this way but, equally, a substantial number of those who read well and widely spend not a few hours doing exactly the same. However, the already weaker and less motivated reader is not helped to improve his reading skills if he is lured by the screen.

'But it is so, and it was so'

Perhaps there was an age when every child read improving stories, learned to be little men and little women and, in due course, good wives (with perhaps an allowable slip into being the naughtiest girl in the school), journeyed to the centre of the earth, followed Flint and Squire Trelawny in search of treasure and looked to the future with great expectations. It was a world of 'God bless the squire and his relations and keep us in our proper stations' and we thanked heaven that the obnoxious Toad was restored to his rightful place in Toad Hall by his faithful Badger and dim-witted Ratty and Mole, whatever he had done. How many times has that scene been acted o'er in recent years? The Whitehead Year 8 list of most widely read books reaches back far into the previous century and bespeaks a world in which the schools had control of students' reading material in a way in which they neither have nor could have in the present day. There are those who think they *should*, not least because, as Rhodes Boyson realized (1975), story is one of the main means by which traditional values are instilled and passed from generation to generation.

But genies are unwilling to be put back into bottles. For good or ill, there has been an explosion in the production of books for young people and young people themselves are often reading much more material that would formerly have been judged adult. In addition, many have the buying power to collect their own hoards of paperbacks. The explosion extends way beyond reading or the concerns about television viewing first expressed in the 1950s: edges and divisions are blurred not only in the choice of fiction reading but in television and video viewing, magazine reading, and computer games playing, each of which now feeds off the other. Reading can never be simply confined between the covers of a book.

Ironically, market forces now rule in reading and in viewing: the consumer is king and the consumer wants Judy Blume and Terry Pratchett, R.L. Stine and Stephen King, Roald Dahl and Sue Townsend. It is admittedly a mixed bag, but who is to say they are wrong? Whatever we may feel about it, this is a more individualistic age with far more choices open to the young in the way they live than previous generations had to face. And the age produces the books. Whilst one registers first the massive change in the most popular texts and the convergence of taste this seems to indicate, we should also be alive to the sheer range and diversity of adolescents' reading which is startling in comparison with the relatively limited reading of previous generations.

The falling away from the standard classics of past generations does not in itself mean a decline in literacy. Vast amounts of reading are going on not only of a wide range of fiction and non-fiction but also of magazines – some of them quite demanding. Of more concern is that we do not seem to have attracted boys to reading in any greater number over the past twenty years or so. The hard core of those who can but do not read is stubbornly there and, of course, it reflects an attitude towards reading prevalent in a large number of adult males. The causes of the problem are not easy to discern but as Maggie Iles (1995) suggests, creating a climate where boys do not see intellectual pursuits as second best to other things with which they wish to fill their lives is something at which we should all, parents and teachers alike, be aiming.

What we do know is that one of the few ways in which we can exert any pressure for change on the situation is through imaginative and informed English teaching which takes account of where the students are in their reading and builds on that foundation. Another is through better library provision and support both in the school and the public sector. Alastair West observed that 'readers are made, not born, and they are made or unmade, largely at school' (West, 1986) and there is a considerable body of evidence, not least his own research, to suggest that much can be done given sufficient support. We are very far from the death of literacy which has been so often announced though the literacy that is emerging may be of a different kind from that with which previous generations were familiar.

6 A personal approach to teaching English

CHRISTINE LAWSON

In this chapter, Christine Lawson draws on her considerable experience – as an advisory teacher, as a Head of English in a large, mixed comprehensive school, and as a school mentor for PGCE English students – in order to present a personal account of the kinds of thinking and activities that constitute successful English teaching.

Learning to teach English

In the early days of my teaching career, teaching was very much a solitary activity. Although you might discuss individual students' progress, or behaviour in the staffroom at break, your own teaching methods were private within the confines of your classroom. There was little open discussion of teaching approaches; as a beginning teacher, I felt it would reflect badly on my professionalism if I admitted I could not cope, or did not know how to teach. After all, I had just graduated and was treated by my colleagues as if I was expected to know how to teach. My teaching experience therefore was gained through a personal, instinctive, process of trial and error based on spontaneous reactions and judgements in the teaching situation.

What I did learn is that there is no one right way to teach English and that the skills of teaching English cannot be acquired overnight. Instead, a degree of sensitivity and flexibility is required in order to accommodate the wide range of factors influencing every teaching situation. Every student is different, with different interests, social backgrounds, personalities and learning needs. It is important to develop perceptive insight into individual learning contexts and be prepared to try a wide range of strategies to cope with an infinite variety of teaching and learning situations, rather than adopting a rigid approach.

I also learned how little use my own specialist knowledge was in terms of teaching the subject to students. Although I could use the conventions of written English with competence, it proved to be an entirely different task teaching students how to use those same skills. The more I tried to explain the intricacies of punctuation, the more aware I became of the inadequacy of my own knowledge. Simple punctuation marks which I used without thinking suddenly became difficult concepts to explain to inexperienced writers. The clarity of every spelling rule I tried to teach was confused by endless exceptions to every rule.

What quickly became apparent was that teaching English was far more complex than I had realized and I did not know how to do it. I therefore began the process of learning by experience, of trial and error, questioning and extending my methodology, beginning to understand how children learn and how I could help them to acquire the skills of using language. Throughout my teaching career, I have come to the conclusion that learning to teach English takes considerable *time* – you need to develop flexibility and sensitivity to the individual learning needs of students; a perceptive and imaginative approach to teaching in the classroom context; and the supportive framework of an extensive range of teaching and learning strategies.

My most memorable impression of my own teacher training is of one lesson for which I had planned a debate on capital punishment. With the enthusiasm of a student keen to try new teaching techniques, I decided to organize the class into small discussion groups, rather than direct the more traditional whole-class debate. My criteria for the selection of groups was crudely based on the quickest and quietest means of students moving desks into a group arrangement. The students went along with this diversion from usual practice very willingly and to my relief were interested in the topic and began their discussions. However, when the class teacher 'just looked in to see how I was doing', he was horrified to see his straight rows of students re-arranged and talking to each other in their discussion groups. After the lesson, he made his disapproval very clear and instructed me not to work in that way with his class in future.

Thus 'prepared' by my teaching practice, I entered the classroom of my first lesson as a teacher of English. With some trepidation regarding the awesome responsibilities of being *an English teacher*, I stood behind the teacher's desk and faced the class. Mustering a confidence which I did not feel, I spoke in a severe, firm voice and instructed my students to write an essay, which they very obligingly proceeded to do (much to my relief). I sat down nervously in the teacher's chair behind the teacher's desk, and wondered what to do next. I remember spending a tranquil hour quietly supervising the rows of 30 heads bent diligently to their task. I also recall a sense of unease and an awareness that something seemed to be lacking; this was too easy and was surely not all that was expected of me as a teacher. However, the students seemed to know what was expected of them and asked me no questions regarding the written task. At the end of the lesson I carried out the other aspect of my teaching role which I knew about; I dutifully collected their exercise books and took them home for marking.

Following the only model of practice which I had encountered, and with no guidance or instruction from the Head of Department, who seemed to have faith that I knew what I was doing, I planned a comprehension exercise for the next lesson, choosing what I perceived to be an interesting extract from the *Secondary Certificate English*. My teaching method was to read the extract to the class, followed by an explanation of how they had to answer the questions which followed and then leaving them once again to their task. I alternated this model of teaching with some vocabulary exercises and spelling tests and this seemed to constitute an acceptable pattern of work.

My teaching methodology was initially formed around this structure of alternating essay writing with comprehension exercises, mixed with vocabulary and spelling for good measure. The methodology was based principally upon objectives of checking students' understanding of the written word through comprehension and vocabulary exercises and encouraging their ability to write accurately and imaginatively. Gradually, however, my sense of dissatisfaction with this kind of teaching began to take shape, formulated around questions and reflections on my practice such as:

- Why am I placing such an emphasis on creative/imaginative writing? Is this likely to be of any benefit to students when they leave school?
- Do students improve their ability to spell, punctuate and use grammar correctly or appropriately through decontextualized exercises from the textbook?
- Were students gaining any benefit from the continuous practice of essay writing, alternating with comprehensions and vocabulary exercises?
- How relevant was what I was teaching them to the actual language skills they would need to use with competence and confidence when they left school?
- Was I giving them sufficient help/instruction in *how* to use language effectively, or was I expecting them to use their own knowledge and initiative to accomplish tasks which I simply instructed them to do?
- Was there more to teaching the skills of English than simply devising interesting tasks to motivate students to write mostly for the purpose of displaying imaginative qualities, or their understanding of texts?

These issues seem somewhat simplistic in hindsight but at the time research into how children acquire and use language was still in its early stages. Most teachers' degree training was literature-based and understanding of theoretical knowledge and research about how children acquire language was in its early stages (for example, the seminal *Language, the Learner and the School*; Barnes *et al.*, 1969).

Most of the development in my own practice, therefore, was as a result of trial and error and a reflective, questioning approach which enabled me to identify certain features of my own practice which seemed to me to be effective. Gradually, as a result of this process, I came to identify certain key issues – key points of focus – that I wanted to concentrate on in my English teaching:

- Motivation of students – recognition of their interests, values, cultures.
- Active involvement of students in learning process – allowing choice.
- Relevance of tasks to students' needs and experiences.
- Differentiation – learning tasks appropriate to level of ability.
- Assessment – positive and constructive; diagnostic comments.
- Importance of praise and encouragement in forming self-esteem.
- Contexts in which students could *use* language.

In the early 1970s, my teaching methods were influenced by a series of course work books called *English Through Experience*. These methods were based on encouraging imaginative writing through sensory experience, and recognizing the value of students' personal response. Students were asked to write 'freely and personally' and to become aware of and react to the world around them through their senses. The teacher's role was to provide a sensory stimulus such as a photograph, intended to trigger a personal memory and provide the impetus to write a story, or poem. Students' writing was praised not only for the power and effectiveness of the imaginative response but also for its degree of sincerity and personal feelings.

This approach led to some exciting lessons in attempts to create 'real', or actual experiences as a stimulus for descriptive, imaginative writing. Several teachers tried the suggested stimulus in *English Through Experience Book 1* for initiating writing about 'Fire' by setting fire to coloured card in a waste bin. The class was expected to watch (usually in silence) as it burned and then describe in writing what they had seen. In order to stimulate my class to some Keatsian autumnal writing, I took them for a delightful autumnal walk in the woodland surrounding the school. It was certainly a 'real' experience but poetic, descriptions of nature were far from the minds of most of the class.

The theory of experiential writing was supported by models of writing from established authors on similar themes and experiences, which resulted in considerable popularity for the *thematic* approach to English. The principle was that students would widen their own vocabulary and writing skills through exposure to examples of writing models, written by professional, published, classical authors around specific themes, such as fear, conflict, friendship or death. Writing tasks were designed to give students practice in using new vocabulary until it became assimilated into their own language repertoire.

An important factor in the development of English teaching methods was the introduction of mixed-ability teaching. Teaching a class of students at different levels of ability meant that it was difficult to maintain the traditional passive teacher-directed format of teaching, in which the teacher stood at the front of the class and instructed all students in the same way to do the same task. New approaches began to be developed based on a more interactive method of teaching, in which the student was involved as an independent learner.

The *English Through Experience* course addressed the problem of differentiation of ability from the point of view of pace. Able students finished preliminary tasks very quickly and therefore needed further tasks. Part Two of the unit of work was designed to offer extension tasks, so that students would 'never be at a loss for something to do':

> In Part Two of every chapter, there will always be plenty to do, plenty to occupy the fastest worker. You can do it while the others are finishing, you can work from it in your spare time, you can do some of it for homework.

The tasks in Part Two were based on involving students as independent learners, offering them a choice of assignments such as library research on the story of Prometheus, or idioms connected with fire, or producing a list of rules for prevention of fire in the home.

There was also clear encouragement of reading for pleasure and enjoyment. Part Three of the course offered a selection of literary and factual extracts linked to the theme of fire and invited students to respond in a personal way by asking if the extract reminded them of anything in their own experience, or if they liked the extract. Although the main emphasis was still essentially a written response, the beginnings of oral discussion can be seen as students were directed to: 'Discuss the pieces with your friends. Do they like the same one as you?'

My own practice was now driven by the conviction that I needed more professional knowledge and understanding of how students learn to use language. I felt that my teaching needed to be more related to the actual needs of language use as a collaborative means of communication, and more directed towards developing the skills which students would need in a variety of situations once they had left school. In order to extend students' linguistic capabilities, I wanted to develop methods which would allow students to practise their language skills in more realistic, relevant contexts rather than decontextualized exercises testing comprehension, correcting spellings, grammar and punctuation and encouraging creative writing.

The next stage in my teaching development was influenced by the work of several national research projects: the National Writing Project, the National Oracy Project, the Reading Survey and LINC (Language in the National Curriculum). The work of these research projects influenced my perceptions both of the *role of the teacher* and of the *teaching strategies* that would be most appropriate. I shall deal with each of these in turn.

The role of the teacher

What emerged from all of the research projects was the need for teachers to adopt a new role in the way they brought about student learning. The research of the National Oracy Project supported the evidence that it was normally the case that the teacher controlled all language in the classroom. The teacher was in charge of spoken language, determining who could speak and for how long. Unsurprisingly, teacher-talk dominated, with students having little opportunity to practise their own language skills, other than answering teacher-initiated questions. It was the teacher who was seen as the arbiter of correct knowledge, praising the 'right' answer and allowing few challenges to the voice of the teacher's knowledge. Similarly, written language was teacher-initiated and teacher-corrected.

Research evidence indicated that students required a sense of ownership in the ways they used language in interactive communicative situations, in order for new learning to take place. Instead of the teacher being perceived as the expert who controls and dominates language use in the classroom, this evidence showed that teachers needed to provide opportunities for students to use spoken and written language as a means of thinking, planning, developing and expressing their own learning:

> to be meaningful, a curriculum has to be enacted by pupils as well as teachers . . . by enact, I mean come together in a meaningful communication, talk, write, read books, collaborate, become angry with others, learn to say and do and how to interpret what others say and do.
>
> (Barnes, 1976)

A collaborative approach to using language relies on a framework of teaching strategies and methodology based on creating planned situations where there is a clear and relevant sense of purpose underlying the learning task and requiring a sense of audience to respond to the outcome, whether spoken or written. This places the teacher in the role of audience, responding as reader and listener to students' learning.

The responsibility of the teacher does not imply a passive acceptance of students' use of language but rather demands that the teacher should move them on beyond the boundaries of their present language repertoire. Progression in language use depends on the function of the teacher as an experienced user of language who can demonstrate particular models of language, provide appropriate examples and give instruction to improve and extend students' understanding of language and how it is used to create meaning. Teachers of English can set an example of experienced language use by acting as readers and writers alongside students. They can demonstrate enthusiasm for reading by taking the opportunity of reading themselves and talking about reading to students. They can write alongside students to demonstrate that adult writers may find it just as difficult to start writing as students and that we also need to use a dictionary, or a spell-checker to check our spellings.

If students are to be provided with genuine opportunities for using language in the classroom, the teacher's function needed to change from the expert – the one who knows – to the facilitator, the one who can provide the teaching context within which the students can learn about using language. The teacher of English should aim to inspire and motivate students, acting as an enthusiastic guide as their students explore new knowledge about language, and try out new language skills.

Teaching strategies

The language skills of speaking, listening, reading and writing are interrelated. The learning context should be planned to create situations in which students are given instruction and practice in using these skills in a variety of situations. The teacher should plan the work based on active involvement of students in deciding upon appropriate language forms to use in a variety of situations. The tasks should have a sense of purpose which is clearly explained to the students and provided with the necessary teaching instruction and models to follow. Students should be directly involved in planning and deciding how to present the task, realizing that the presentation format will be determined by the audience to whom it is to be presented.

Initially, I introduce a broad theme, or text upon which to structure teaching and learning. I use a variety of strategies to engage students' interest and motivate them in the learning activity. I involve them by asking open questions which require them to formulate a view on the topic and not simply to express opinions of 'right' or 'wrong'. The vehicle for investigating and using language can be text-based, such as prose, poetry or drama. However, it can also be non-literary, or media texts such as a series of adverts, a television programme, a selection of magazines or newspapers.

Through a series of strategies based on involving students in reading and direct discussion of the various text, we then move to a consideration of the format through which students can demonstrate their learning and practise the skills they are developing. This may be in the form of a written assignment, which will involve consideration of the presentation format of the finished piece of writing. Would a booklet form be appropriate, or a poster, or a report structure? Should the language used be formal or informal in style? Who are we writing to? Who are we writing for? Is there an intended audience beyond the teacher? Is this audience real or imagined?

The final outcome need not be in written form. It may take the form of enactment through playscript or improvisation. It may be in a media format, such as using a video camera to produce a visual presentation, making a radio programme, a magazine or newspaper. Information technology resources will be used wherever appropriate to enhance the quality of the finished product.

The sense of audience can be created in several ways. The teacher need not be the sole responder to the final presentation. Students can present plays and spoken performances to a variety of audiences, other students in the classroom, other teaching groups, students from other schools, house assemblies and parents. Written work can be read by groups of students as part of a writing circle; poems, plays and stories can be published in school magazines and sent as entries to competitions. Students' writing can be published as an anthology and distributed to a wider audience.

Eventually, the teacher should evaluate the work in terms of students' learning, to determine whether progress has been made, new skills learned, or old skills reinforced. This can be recorded in a variety of ways. Initially, the student should be involved in the evaluation process and assess their strengths and weaknesses. Positive achievements should be noted and areas of weakness targeted for further practice. A notebook can be kept by the students in which to record ways of improving.

The official assessment in terms of Key Stage 3 or GCSE. Criteria should be recorded in the teacher's mark book, bearing in mind a positive, constructive analysis on a piece of work, or direct comment to the student is of more value than a letter or number grade. This is particularly evident in the case of low attainers who may be easily discouraged by low grades, if they have worked to the best of their ability. Equally, some students will thrive on being high achievers and are motivated by successful grades. The decision as to whether to inform students of their achievement according to external criteria should depend on the teacher's judgement of the level of self-esteem of individual students.

In learning how to use language effectively, students must be actively engaged in using language. The teacher of English must create opportunities within the classroom situation which enable students to think through language and to express their learning through the language modes of speaking, listening, reading and writing. A variety of strategies have been developed which encourage students as active meaning-makers, using language to go beyond the literal in investigating how language works and is used as a form of thinking and communication.

Speaking and listening

It is important that all students are enabled to use spoken language fluently and competently as a means of making and expressing meaning. However, in a class of 30 students, classroom dynamics often inhibit many students from participating in spoken activities. A classroom situation which is dominated by the structure of teacher-initiated questions will generally result in the same few students responding each time. They will be the students confident enough to speak in front of their peers, without being afraid of being corrected or praised by the teacher.

The process of listening and responding to the spoken word is complex and inexperienced users of spoken language often need time to assimilate the words, work out the meaning and formulate a response. However, research has shown that most teachers allow little time for students to answer before moving quickly on to the student who has an answer ready. Most students under the pressure of this type of question–answer structure simply switch off, or carry on an inner form of response within their own heads, whereby they acknowledge only to themselves whether they know the answer the teacher is expecting, or not. This is not a useful way of determining the extent of an individual student's knowledge or the extent to which they are participating in the lesson.

Many teachers complain about inattentive students, who do not appear to be listening and become frustrated by students' apparent inability to follow instructions which they have clearly explained. However, many adults also switch off from listening in situations where one person is dominating the spoken form of communication, particularly if the speaker is boring, or speaks in a monotonous voice.

The teacher needs to bring about a situation in which all students are encouraged to contribute their views and opinions. The teacher must build up an ethos of respecting the views of other people, being prepared to listen and accept with a tolerant attitude that other people's views may be different. Consideration of the personal aspects of using spoken language should be taken into account, showing sensitivity to the needs of individual students.

Creating a classroom ethos in which all students feel comfortable about using spoken language can be achieved through careful grouping of students and a range of teaching strategies based on the research of the National Oracy Project.

Organization of students into groups can be determined by the teaching intention and knowledge of individual students' learning needs. Some students will benefit from gaining confidence working in friendship groups. Other students may need to be challenged by working with students of a higher ability than themselves. Sometimes mixed-ability groups are appropriate but in other teaching situations you may want students of similar ability to work together. There may also be the opportunity for students to work in mixed age groups, single gender groups or specific interest groups. Teachers may strategically group students according to more dominant/reticent personalities, or sometimes in random groupings. The size of the group can also vary from pairs, to small groups of three to six, or a larger grouping of half a class.

It is important to make a distinction between allowing students an uncontrolled voice in the classroom and organizing structured learning opportunities through which they can use language as a means of thinking and expressing their thoughts. The following strategies are ways of structuring talk for learning in the classroom.

Talk partners

This strategy can be used to include all students in a whole-class discussion situation. Instead of asking a question or posing a thought for discussion in order to elicit views to start a topic, ascertain what the student knows. Ask the question but explain that you do not want hands-up answers. Instead, allow time for all members of the class to discuss the question with the person sitting next to them – a talk partner. Discuss the topic for a given time and then ask for feedback into the whole-class situation. Students will then have had a chance to think through their views, gaining practice in expressing their ideas to one person and becoming more prepared to offer spoken response in a large group situation.

Non-threatening response

In a whole-class situation where it is appropriate to expect a response from each student, ask for a one-word or one-sentence response. Most students feel able to contribute at least a brief response, particularly if they are allowed the opportunity to 'pass' to allow more thinking time.

Brainstorm

This is a popular method of initiating a topic and generating ideas and opinions. It is based on free-flow association of ideas where students offer words, phrases, ideas in connection with a particular subject. This may begin as a whole-class activity based on voluntary responses or short word, phrase or sentence from each individual. The teacher may simply receive these as oral offerings without discussion, or record them on the board for future reference. Small groups can then be formed to brainstorm the topic, or to select a particular idea to follow through. The idea is to collect quick, short responses, valuing the contribution of all members of the group.

Although this activity can be entirely oral, it provides a useful focus if students write their responses as a graffiti board. This involves using felt pens to record words and phrases on large sheets of sugar paper or A3. For example, students can make a graffiti board of unfamiliar words and phrases in *Journey's End* leading to a discussion of language change. Or they can collect words illustrating a literary aspect relating to characters or themes, for example collecting words connected with light/darkness in *Romeo and Juliet*. These initial collections of words and phrases can then be used as the basis for further discussion.

Two's and four's

In this activity students work in pairs (based on friendship or ability criteria). They may discuss their views on a particular issue and then move on to join another pair. Each pair explains the main points of their discussion and then widens the discussion within the group of four. A further variation is that in each pair, each person must explain the other person's point of view to the new pair.

Jigsaw

This structure is particularly useful for research projects, such as 'Shakespeare's Life and Times'. The class of students is divided into smaller groups of five or six. These are known as the 'home' group. The research project is then divided into sections and each member of the home group chooses a section to research. The class is then re-formed into 'specialist' research groups, i.e. all students researching 'Theatres in Shakespeare's Times' form a working group. After a specified amount of time, which could vary from two or three lessons to 2–3 weeks, depending on the activity, the specialist groups re-form as the original home groups. Each specialist member of the home group then reports back on their research. The home group then incorporates all information into a final presentation format, which could be an information booklet, or a video/radio programme, etc.

Envoy

This structure is based on the sharing of ideas and active discussion. The class is divided into groups with a particular assignment. This could be to discuss a poem, an aspect of a novel, or play they are studying, or any issue. After a given amount of time, the group should summarize the key point of their debate, issues arising, questions remaining unanswered. One person from the group is chosen to act as envoy. All the envoys move groups and report the discussion of their original group to the new group. This may continue until all envoys have visited all groups, although this is time-consuming and may not be necessary, depending on the task. The envoy then returns to the original group with new knowledge gained, questions answered, different views.

Listening triads

This is an interesting structure developing listening skills in particular. Students are organized in groups of three to carry out an interview activity. This could be the nurse in *Romeo and Juliet* interviewing Romeo to determine whether he genuinely loves Juliet. Each student takes one of the following roles: speaker, questioner, recorder. The speaker explains or comments on a particular topic. The questioner seeks clarification of any points not understood. The recorder makes notes and at the end of the specified time gives a report of the conversation.

Reading

Encouraging students to become readers is increasingly difficult in today's multimedia world. They have access to a far wider range of leisure facilities, including television, video and computer games than ever (see Chapter 5). In contrast, the mechanical act of reading the printed word in books is often slow and tedious. Many students are put off reading by the slowness of the procedure, the often uninspiring nature of the texts they are required to read and the much hated 'reading around the class'. A lot of energy is expended on simply decoding the literal meaning of the printed word. There is often little understanding or capacity to make inferences below the surface meaning of the words.

Encouraging students to read for pleasure and to become life-long readers requires the cultivation of a reading ethos, of teacher reading alongside students and promoting an interchange of opinions about reading, allowing students to explore their own reading interests, making recommendations as an adult reader and demonstrating your own enthusiasm for reading. A wide range of reading materials should be available for independent reading, such as prose, poetry, drama, leaflets, magazines and newspapers. Access to a range of thesauruses, dictionaries and language reference books should also be available.

The difficulty of the actual reading process means that many students are passive readers, whose time is taken up only with the surface meaning of text – readers at this stage are not able to penetrate to the underlying levels of writers' intentions and uses of language in order to create effect and response in the reader. Our aim as teachers of English should be to develop articulate readers who question the text, in order to construct their own meaning and form a critical evaluation of what the writer has written.

A series of strategies was developed through research, particularly by Lunzer and Gardner (1979), encouraging an active study of the text through a variety of problem-solving activities. Readers were required to use thinking and reasoning skills to make deductions and infer underlying meaning, discussing, reshaping and questioning in order to construct their own understandings. These strategies are known as DARTS (Directed Activity Related to Text) and are designed to develop skills of reasoning and self-questioning in understanding the written word.

Cloze procedure

Select a section of text, photocopy and delete certain words (every tenth word) either using Tipp-Ex or retyping, leaving equal-length spaces. Read the passage aloud and share with students your predictions for the missing words, explaining your reasoning. The deleted words could be content words (nouns, verbs, adjectives, adverbs); structural words (conjunctions, pronouns, articles, prepositions) or words connected to a particular theme (key words in the balcony scene of *Romeo and Juliet*).

Students then predict the most appropriate words to fill in the gaps, either individually or in groups. This task can be differentiated according to the needs of students. A jumbled list of possible words could be supplied to support less-able students. Predicting the missing words and then comparing their version with the original provides the need to reason and understand the function of words within a sentence and how writers construct language to create meaning. Students can also be involved in choosing words to delete in preparing a piece of text for fellow students.

Sequencing

This is a popular strategy and again students can be involved in preparing the materials. Basically, a piece of appropriate text, a prose extract or a complete poem is cut up into sections and stuck onto card. The students then rearrange the segments, reconstructing the text into a logical sequence. This strategy demonstrates understanding of narrative structure and the ability to infer meaning using clues in the text, for example rhyme schemes in poetry indicate a clear structure and help students to understand how writers shape language to create poetic effects.

Prediction

In this activity students are asked to make predictions, using the text to justify their comments. The aim is to make judgements about the text supported by inferences relating to themes, characters and narrative structure. Students can be asked to predict what a particular book may be about from the front cover or the publisher's blurb. During the course of reading, students may be stopped at certain points to predict the likely outcome, basing their judgement on noted features of character, theme and characteristics of genre.

Questioning the text

The whole point of making meaning is that understanding should be the product of students' own thinking and effort, rather than something imposed by the teacher. This activity therefore places the students in the role of questioner, actively interrogating the text themselves. It increases student motivation as they are identifying the questions which they genuinely want to be answered.

Students are asked to read a piece of text and make a note of any aspects they do not understand. Using a highlighter pen is very effective to highlight words, phrases and ideas that they do not understand. These should then be formulated by students into questions for discussion, either using the Two's into Four's structure, or teacher working with whole class. Students also enjoy devising their own questions for other students to answer, especially in a quiz format.

There are a variety of strategies which can be used as ways into texts, to motivate and encourage students' reading (see Benton and Fox 1985, *Twenty Four Things to do with a Book*).

Teacher reading

Initially, if starting a new text with students, I read the first chapter to them. Students enjoy listening to stories and it provides a model of an experienced reader. My intention is to engage their interest in the text, encourage them by taking them part way into the story. I may ask for students to volunteer as readers, or suggest students read only one sentence, or paragraph. A lively way of encouraging students to participate in whole class reading sessions is by asking them to be a character. The book is then read as a playscript, with students breaking into the narrative and reading in character.

Shared reading

Students can be organized into reading groups. The groups can be organized according to mixed ability, appointing better readers to act as reading supporters of less-able students and helping to fill in words for less-able readers. Groups of similar high ability can speed away, following a guidesheet of activities related to their understanding of the text. Less-able readers may read an edited version of the story, concentrating on key scenes identified by the teacher.

Supported reading

Less-able readers may have the support of a classroom assistant, or a sixth-form helper. They find enlarged photocopies of extracts from the text very useful, as well as listening to taped versions. They can also be taught how to skim-read the text in order to gain a quick overall impression of the story. Many struggling readers give up because the slow pace of decoding every word is too tedious and difficult for them to sustain interest in the story.

Individual reading

Many students prefer to read on their own. Quiet space should be provided if possible in the classroom or the library. Set aside a time for individual concentrated reading to develop the habit of spending time reading. A variety of acronyms have been developed to describe independent reading:

ERIC: Everyone Reading In Class
DEAR: Drop Everything And Read
USSR: Uninterrupted Sustained Silent Reading
SCAR: Sit Comfortably And Read

Dramatic readings

Students prepare and practise reading extracts which demonstrate their ability to read with expression, creating mood and atmosphere, reading in appropriate characters' voices. The whole text can be divided up and each group given a section to present to the whole class.

Drama is a close ally of English as it provides ideal opportunities for creating contexts using language. The techniques of drama provide a range of interactive opportunities for students to explore the use of language and to study how language is used to create meaning through character and dramatic situation in human experience. Drama strategies are often very effective in motivating students and helping them to interpret character, theme and setting. Drama involves students in active consideration of the texts and allows them to present their understanding in interesting ways.

Here is a selection of well-known strategies that I personally have found immensely effective in the classroom, to a large extent based on Jonathan Neeland's suggestions in *Structuring Drama Work* (1990):

Games and ice breakers

There are several examples of games which can be used to break down inhibitions in group work and to support group dynamics. Their most important function is to develop a sense of trust within the group so that each individual feels secure enough to make a valid personal contribution to the work of the group. There are several good examples to be found in G. Rawlins and J. Rich's *Look, Listen and Trust – a framework for learning through drama* (1985).

Still-image/tableaux

This involves selecting a part of the text and depicting the scene by using themselves to create a picture which represents the key feature of the situation. They must present a silent frozen representation in which they do not move or speak. For example, they could choose to represent the scene on the beach from *Lord of the Flies* when Simon emerges from the forest. The rest of the class should look carefully at the image, consider their interpretation of the scene and work out what the image is representing in terms of character and action.

This can be followed by 'thought – tracking', in which the characters are brought to life. This is achieved by one person from the audience selecting a character in the image and gently touching them on the shoulder. They may either ask a question to clarify their understanding of the situation, or the character in the image may speak one word/phrase/sentence which represents the thoughts of the character in that situation. The whole image may be brought to life by asking each person in the class to speak in turn, saying one sentence which encapsulates the key features of the narrative sequence, what's happening in the image.

Hot-seating

This is a useful device for exploring characters' motivation and finding out information about characters. One person chooses to represent a character, for example Simon in *Lord of the Flies*. The other students then devise questions relevant to determining how the character feels at a particular moment and finding out further background details. The character must answer the questions in role, relating the answers to their interpretation of the text.

A day in the life

This is a popular structure for reconstructing sequences illustrating events from characters' lives. It can be based on textual, or imaginary characters and situations. Use still images or a series of improvisations to explore events and influences in a character's life.

Reportage

In this activity, students take on the role of reporters in order to represent textual events through journalistic or dramatic conventions. It could take the form of a documentary news programme reporting the tragic death of young lovers in *Romeo and Juliet* or investigative journalism: 'who was responsible for their deaths?' This structure includes interviews with witnesses in role as appropriate characters from the text.

Improvisation

This places students in a similar situation to characters in the text. They are required to imagine themselves in a particular situation and to behave in ways appropriate to the situation as it develops. The situation could be an exploration of a scene from a text, as in the scene between Juliet and her parents when she refuses to marry Paris or an imaginary modern version of a similar parent–child situation.

Play-making

This activity can be based on reconstructing events from the text, for example re-enacting the trial scene from *To Kill a Mockingbird* can be particularly effective. The same situation could be imagined in a different context, for example a modern version. Alternatively, students could explore an imaginary version of the same experience, writing and presenting their playscript to an audience. Themes of genre can be explored through students devising their own versions of popular TV programmes, or devising the next episode of a typical soap.

Writing

Writing in school for many students consists in laborious handwriting, copying information from text books or note-taking dictated by the teacher or written on the board. Different subject teachers may have differing expectations regarding the content and style of the written work but the main emphasis tends to be on features such as neat handwriting, tidy presentation and correct spellings. The focus is often on legibility and accuracy rather than clarity of expression in terms of coherence of ideas. Handwriting is therefore perceived by students as a mechanical act of transcription, using writing to note information and knowledge which has to be recalled for examination or test purposes.

In everyday life, we are more likely to use writing not only to remember things but also to organize our ideas, reflect on experience, communicate with others, clarify ideas, report events, share opinions, entertain, inform and persuade. We use a variety of forms to transfer our inner thoughts to an explicit recorded form, ranging from notes and diagrams, to diaries and formal reports. If we are writing to inform, or entertain, we choose from a variety of literary and non-literary formats: plays, poetry, posters or leaflets.

We vary the style and format of our writing depending on who we are writing for – our own private perusal, a friend, a member of the family, a business colleague. The style of language used depends very much on the formality of the purpose for writing and its intended audience.

As experienced writers, we are aware that we need certain conditions in order to write effectively. Some of us may need peace and quiet, whilst others prefer music playing in the background. We need to have access to resources such as dictionaries, a thesaurus, a word-processor or a spell-checker in order to make writing easier. As writers, we appreciate a response to what we have written and usually prefer this to be constructive and tactful.

Good classroom practice should try and recreate the same working conditions we prefer as writers for students writing in the classroom. They should be aware of a clear sense of purpose for writing and they need to realize that as writers in control of their writing it is they who should decide upon the format and style which is most appropriate for the intended readers of the writing.

Students are more motivated if they are asked to write with a genuine say in what they are to write about and if there is a genuine purpose for writing. For instance, teachers need to help students identify situations where they can write to appropriate people – such as local politicians – to express their own views on genuine local issues. They can be encouraged to write to newspapers, magazines and television as an outlet for their views. Writing is easier if it is based on some form of reality, so if students are writing in the form of a report, or survey, it is more relevant if they have actually carried out the research, for example a survey of the popularity of school meals is a popular topic.

Principles of the writing process

The National Writing Project carried out several action research projects investigating effective practice in teaching students about writing. Their research identified the structure of the developmental writing process as:

1 Motivation to write	6 Revising
2 Brainstorming	7 Editing
3 Reflection	8 Writing final copy
4 Making preliminary notes	9 Publishing/display
5 Drafting	10 Response from readers.

In the initial stages of motivation, the teacher can use a range of stimuli to encourage students to write and organize opportunities for students to talk through their ideas and plan their writing in collaboration with other writers, or independently. Wherever possible, students should choose the content, or focus of their writing and the format in which they wish to present their response.

Drafting should be seen as an integral part of the writing process and models can be used to show writer's such as Wilfred Owen and his drafting of *Dulce et Decorum Est*. The term 'drafting' should be explained and demonstrated to students so that it is perceived as a process of editing and refining ideas, restructuring and improving clarity of expression, rather than the narrow perception of first 'rough' and then 'neat' copy model of drafting.

As facilitator of students' writing, I intervene at various points in the writing process. I do this through individual, or group tutorial sessions, in which I offer my advice on various aspects of their writing. I am available as a consultant editor and proofreader during the writing process. However, in a class of 30 students, it is difficult to spend enough time with each individual. It is necessary therefore to make it clear that the teacher is not the only person who can read their writing and make helpful comments.

Students enjoy working in writing circles, reading their work to trusted members of the peer group for comment. As teacher, I provide them with a guide to direct their comments appropriately. Students are usually very careful in their response and offer helpful advice to their fellow writers. As students they often find it easier to accept a friendly comment pointing out aspects of a piece of writing that might be improved, rather than a professional comment from the teacher.

The ethos of the writing classroom is to develop a sense of pride in creating an effective piece of writing. This is best achieved in terms of direct response as reader to the writing. Students are pleased by specific praise, rather than platitudes of 'that's good'. I comment specifically on features of their writing which I have enjoyed or are particularly effective in their use of writing techniques. One of my highest accolades is when I read students' work to the rest of the class based on the criteria of the 'spine-tingling' factor: a piece of writing which genuinely impresses me and engages my feelings.

Developing writers thrive on praise and encouraging comments, rather than on derogatory comments, or criticisms focused mainly on errors of spelling, punctuation and grammar. As writers they benefit from their writing being read by a variety of audiences and presented in lively and interesting ways. For example, students can publish an anthology of their writing, or present a reading of their writing for friends, parents and governors. If they have written stories for younger children, they can visit the local primary school and read their stories to a live audience. There are always writing competitions encouraging young writers and most people enjoy seeing their name in print, or receiving recognition of their creativity. Above all, I aim to promote a lively active spirit of pleasure and pride in students as independent writers.

Working with Year 7

I shall, finally, try to illustrate some of the strategies I have been talking about by briefly outlining two examples of work I like to use with Year 7 classes. I shall begin with some of the activities which I use in the first few lessons, and then illustrate some of the approaches I would take later on, when studying a novel with such a class.

I like to begin working with a new Year 7 class with work based on an autobiographical theme. This provides a secure foundation for getting to know individual students and forming patterns of working within the class.

As the class is newly formed, most of the students will not know each other; they may be nervous and apprehensive on their first day in secondary education. Ice-breaker name games are ideal to begin breaking down inhibitions and building relationships. I often ask each individual to say their first name and then think of an adjective which they could put in front to describe themselves, starting with the same letter of their first name, i.e. Crazy Christine, Delightful David.

I like to use the jigsaw approach to group work at this early stage. Dividing the class first of all according to different primary school groups, I start with home groups of five or six, and after they have chatted for a while I reform the groups to consist of representatives from different primary schools. In the new groups, each student tells the other students about their primary school experience and what they will miss most. They discuss what they are looking forward to most in their new school. After about 20–25 minutes, students return to their home group and report what they have learned from other groups. After further discussion time, the teacher can draw the group together by asking for report-back. I then write up on the board a list of things students will miss about primary school and what they are looking forward to in secondary school. This activity may need to be adapted according to the number of primary schools attended by students; one can adapt this idea by forming home groups according to different criteria, e.g. primary school teachers, or areas where students live.

Talking

I initiate discussion by asking what makes each person an individual. I allow 5–10 minutes talking time with a 'talk partner' and then ask if anyone would like to share any reflections with the rest of class. I give a demonstration of this, talking about myself as an individual, based around a possession which I have brought in from home. Ask each student to bring in a possession which they feel represents them as an individual for the next lesson. Organize students into supportive friendship groups of approximately 10 students, not too small, to provide friendly audience for talk. Set clear expectations that students will listen attentively to each other.

Reading stimulus

I provide a wide range of texts, literary and non-literary based on autobiographical writing, and use a mixture of teacher reading, individual and shared reading. Students can make a selection of their favourite pieces, talk about their selections in small groups, and make an anthology.

Writing

Focusing on personal writing and autobiography, I involve students in a choice of subject and format of presentation. This could be a passport giving details of the student's life, a poster of photographs and explanations, a diary format, 'A Day or Year In the Life of . . . Edited Highlights'. There are endless possibilities and students always have ideas of their own for this.

Studying a text: The Boy Who Was Afraid by Armstrong Sperry

This is a text which I choose to read with Year 7 students as a starting point for a range of language learning activities. It is a story based in the South Seas and is intended to extend students' awareness of other cultures. I also choose it to motivate boys as readers and to challenge gender stereotypes through the main character, a boy who is indeed afraid. The theme of a young person facing danger and adversity, learning something about themselves and proving themselves to others is universal and appeals both to boys and girls. There are several exciting, dramatic incidents in the story to sustain reading interest and motivation.

I begin by using a prediction exercise, asking students to say what they think the story might be about and where it might be set, based merely on the title and the front of the book. This helps me to gauge their level of awareness about other cultures.

To stimulate interest and engage all students in the text, I then read the first chapter, demonstrating and talking about techniques I am using to vary the tone of my voice to add expression and variation to the narration. My intention is to guide students into the story and leave them wanting to read on for themselves. Taking into account the different levels of reading ability within the class, I organize students into various reading activities:

- Shared student reading in groups based on a selection of criteria: some of the same ability, some of mixed ability. All groups have a structured reading guide, stopping them at various points in the story to discuss aspects of plot, setting and character.
- In group reading, each student can choose how much they want to read, to the level of their own ability and self-confidence as readers – sentence/ paragraph/page. All students are expected to act as prompts and help with pronouncing words.

I will also make use of the following drama strategies:

Hot-seating

Select one student from each group to represent Mafatu at the point at which he decides to leave the island. The other members of the group devise questions to ask him about why he wants to leave the island. This can lead to an em-pathetic piece of writing in character. The students can write as if they are Mafatu and describe their thoughts as they leave the island.

Improvisation
In groups, or pairs, students role-play the final scene when Mafatu returns to the island and is welcomed by his father. They improvise what they think they would say to each other. Each group, or pair presents their version to the rest of the class as audience. This can then be written up in playscript form.

Still-images
The students devise a series of still pictures which depict the main events of Mafatu's experiences. They use thought-tracking to explore Mafatu's feelings at various stages, showing the changes in his character. Each group can work on the story as a whole narrative structure, or can be given a particular scene to prepare.

Research
I use the jigsaw strategy to structure the research, organizing students into home and specialist groups to research information on the South Seas. I will also put students in role as anthropologists/investigative journalists research in order to produce a report or TV style documentary on the South Seas. This approach provides opportunities for getting the students to use the library and CD-ROM facilities.

Word collections
In small groups, students collect unfamiliar words from the text. They re-search meanings of words and produce a glossary for future readers.

Descriptive writing
Choose a descriptive scene, such as the storm scene. I photocopy the extract and read it aloud to the students. They then use highlighter pens or pencil underlining to identify words which make a strong impression upon them. On this basis, we are able to have a substantial discussion about the effectiveness of this descriptive writing. Alternatively, I might photocopy the extract, delete adjectives and then ask students to make their own guesses about appropriate words. We then compare these with the original text, leading to a discussion about how to use language for descriptive effect. This can lead into students' own descriptive writing, for example: 'Remember a time when you felt as afraid as Mafatu.'

Media
The setting of the book provides opportunities for the study of the kind of per-suasive language that is used in travel brochures. I would encourage students to

collect examples of travel brochures and through these study techniques of advertising and persuasive language. Students would then create their own travel brochures attracting tourists to the South Seas, or their home environment.

Narrative re-telling

I will give each student a section of the story to prepare. I then organize the class in story-telling circle. Each student, in role as an appropriate character, tells their part of the story in five sentences. Students are in role as individual characters and as the villagers listening to Mafatu's adventure. This leads to students' own adventure stories of being stranded on a desert island. They can design their own dream island, draw a map of it and write the specifications which they would send to a designer.

Principles and procedures for teaching English: a summary

Underlying all those approaches to teaching English which I have mentioned in this chapter, there are certain principles and procedures which I try to take into account in all that I do as an English teacher. Naturally, it is not always easy to bear such a range of considerations in mind at all times, but the fact is that principles which have grown out of day-to-day practice do continue to be both relevant and feasible.

Planning

- Establish teaching intention
- Select appropriate teaching strategies
- Prepare stimulus material/resources

Teaching input

- Initiate topic/introduce and explain area of study
- Ask what students already know
- Motivate – engage student interest/involvement
- Organize students into appropriate groupings
- Instruct in new aspects of learning
- Set up learning situation
- Study models examples

Process

- Discuss assignment with students
- Offer help to groups, or individuals
- Listen/talk to students about their work
- Encourage, praise, support

- Provide access to library
- Use word-processors and other IT resources

Response

- Watch and listen to final presentation
- Read finished written work
- Respond positively
- Avoid platitudes – offer genuine impressions
- Point out and discuss effective use of language
- Suggest ways in which to improve
- Challenge with extended thinking
- Extend learning with new knowledge
- Public response – extend to new audiences

Follow-up

- Reflect on assignment with student
- Evaluate strengths and weaknesses
- Set learning targets for next assignment

Assessment

- Positive constructive analysis on spoken and written work
- Oral and written comments direct to students
- Award grade according to: (1) Criteria understood by students and (2) Key Stage 3/GCSE criteria

I think of these principles as being very specifically concerned with English teaching, but as I read them through now I realize that they could apply equally well to the teaching of any subject. This suggests to me at least, that the job of the English teacher is above all about doing whatever is necessary to generate students' involvement and understanding in their learning, rather than about any specific or favoured kinds of subject content.

7 A beginning teacher's perspective

KATHY OXTOBY

In this chapter, Kathy Oxtoby, a PGCE English student, explores some of the different perspectives on English teaching that she has come across during the course of her initial teacher training, and discusses her own feelings about the job.

The Introduction to my PGCE English course booklet promised to help me through the transition from student to teacher of English by making me 'explore different (and sometimes contradictory) perspectives on the teaching of English'. There are times, I must admit, when I think I might have preferred someone just to tell me quite straightforwardly (a) what to teach, (b) how to teach it and (c) what to do when the children did not want to learn it. But they did not, and I guess they never will because English teaching really is quite a confusing business: the more people I talked to, and the more things I read, and the more I tried things out for myself in the classroom, the more I realized that this is not something you can wrap up in one short year.

In this chapter, I will sketch out just a few of the different perspectives I came across during this last year about what English teaching is for, what it ought to be for, and what the best ways of doing it might be. In doing so, I will report some of the things that teachers and students have told me about how they see the subject, and what the best ways of teaching it are, before finally trying to make sense of my own feelings about the job.

The teachers

I spent a good deal of time in my PGCE year working in a large English department in quite a big provincial comprehensive school. The teachers that I had the good fortune to work with and learn from during that time – especially my mentor – were helpful, friendly and all very good at their jobs. But that does not mean that the kind of advice they gave me, when I sat them down and asked them to tell me about how each of them saw the job of English teaching, managed to clear up my confusions about what ought to go on. One of the first things I was told, for a start, did very little to ease initial feelings of inadequacy:

> 'English is free from the confines of other text-bound subjects and as a result the English teacher is required to have a wider knowledge than any other teacher and must be prepared to talk about literally any topic.'

(Dave)

I was, perhaps, more encouraged by the following, even if I did not exactly know what it meant:

> 'I like students to feel ownership of their work and I see my own role as a guider and facilitator rather than a dictator.'

(Adam)

I certainly went along with the idea, especially in the early days of the course, that I was not going to be any kind of dictator. In fact, I rather suspect I had thought I would not even have to be a *teacher*, exactly – I rather preferred the idea of being a sort of helpful friend, without actually having to play any artificial role just because that was what everyone else did. I do not believe I ever became a dictator, but now I think I can handle being a teacher. For me, it was a matter of discovering that it is possible to take responsibility for students' learning without having to act like an alien. But I am still not sure if I know what 'ownership of their work' means, and I certainly do not want anyone calling me names like 'facilitator.'

In a way I was equally anxious about the following, although it certainly did fit certain ideas I had about teaching in general:

> 'As English teachers I believe that we have a unique responsibility to develop students' sensitivity and also to be sensitive to their needs. In this sense we have a pastoral role. The personal nature of English means that worries, fears and anxieties are sometimes reflected in the work produced by a student and as a result the English teacher can perhaps view classes more clearly as being made up of unique individuals.'

(Alison)

I really do not know about this, now the year is over and I am asking myself if this is how I want to spend the rest of my life. I certainly liked the vast majority of the students I taught, and enjoyed their company. It was a pleasure getting to know them as individuals, and I am sure there is no subject like English for being able to do that. But I am not sure if I want to see English teaching as a pastoral role, and I really do think that it ought to be more about literacy than sensitivity. But it is difficult to disagree with such a position without seeming rather heartless and insensitive yourself.

I was rather more encouraged by this very different point of view, on the other hand:

'If I had the opportunity to redefine English in terms of what goes on the time-table I would advocate the teaching of language across the curriculum and for 'literature' to be classed as cultural studies. I believe that we need to get away from the idea of 'Englishness' and 'literary heritage.' Teachers should be able to offer the study of a variety of texts rather than operating within the confines of a canon of literature.'

(Jenny)

I liked the idea of redefining the subject, because that makes things clearer, at least. Certainly, my own experience as a student, and out in the world of work as a journalist, had already sent me towards a greater enthusiasm for that kind of cultural studies, non-traditional view of what should be studied in English lessons. Jenny was not alone in this respect, which I found encouraging:

'One of my major concerns regarding the new National Curriculum is that it does not recognise the value of Media Study. Teachers have a responsibility to look closely at media language in terms of both its creativity and power to persuade – it is essential that we increase students awareness of all aspects of language.'

(Simon)

Indeed, the department was well resourced and supported opportunities for media work. But, as the earlier references to developing sensitivity suggest, this was not a universally accepted view. For the most part, though, it was not a question of one kind of English teaching or another that was being advocated, so much as the need to take on multiple tasks with equal skill:

'What we call English I think of as being two subjects; the combined study of language and literature and a 'service' geared towards ensuring that communication and understanding is achieved in other areas of the National Curriculum.'

(Adam)

All the teachers were unanimous, at least, in their frustration at having to satisfy the mass of curriculum and exam syllabus requirements that filled every shelf in the work-room. They all clearly felt that some of these requirements actively got in the way of the kind of teaching they wished to do:

'I believe that a combination of individual and collaborative learning is vital in the English class in order to make learning as active as possible. I constantly look to achieve a balance between reading, writing, speaking and listening which I teach through the medium of literature. It is my intention that every year group should experience one major novel or play, poetry and media analysis. Unfortunately the restrictions of the new orders where pre-twentieth century texts dominate and the demands of SATS and GCSE preparation leave little time to achieve the right balance of fiction, non-fiction, poetry and media work.'

(Dave)

Given my own increasing interest, as the year progressed, in learning how to help children become better writers, I was also confused by what seemed to me to be the rather open-ended guidance I received on how to do this:

'My personal feeling about knowledge about language is that whilst recognising that there is a place for formal language teaching I believe that it is more appropriate to place grammar in context, for example if a student's story lacks punctuation I would want them to re-examine their work in order to correct mistakes. Formal language teaching should be individualized to be at its most meaningful and there are few aspects of language that I would attempt to teach separately at secondary school level – I would hope that basic grammar issues have already been dealt with at primary school.'

(Adam)

The general feeling about grammar was that it should be dealt with in the context of a general lesson rather than a separate issue in 'blackboard bold'. One English teacher commented that having tried various approaches to language over the years, he has now opted to make grammar as fun as possible at Key Stage 3 and uses more serious worksheets by Year 10. He also aims to have one lesson a week at Key Stage 4 devoted to improving students' writing capabilities. I could see the point of this, but it still worried me because there seemed to me to be so few guarantees that certain aspects of writing accurately would ever get taught.

I realized in the end, in fact, that it is genuinely difficult for teachers to *generalize* about how they do their job. I do think that most of these remarks are perfectly fair representations of how these teachers did see their jobs, but in terms of what I could learn from working with these people, I actually found it far more useful whenever these unfailingly kind and helpful teachers gave me specific advice and guidance in response to my questions about particular bits of teaching, or the needs of particular students.

Students' views of English teaching

On the other hand, I did find even the generalizations of the students that I spoke to about similar issues to be extremely perceptive and revealing. I asked them about things like how they saw the subject, what they felt they learnt in English, and what they would *like* to learn; and I got them also to talk to me about what English lessons were like for them, and how they perceived the teachers.

As a way of trying to get at their views of what English was really about, I asked a variety of students, for a start, to tell me what alternative names they might give the subject. Some of their answers struck me as being surprisingly sophisticated:

'An alternative name for "English lessons" would be "life understanding" because it builds your personality so you can understand life.'

(Year 9 student)

'I think "English" should be called "learning the basic knowledge you need to live". It makes it sound more important than just "English" but it would be a bit difficult to fit it on our timetables.'

(Year 10 student)

'A preferable term for "English" would be the understanding and the art of communication. "English" is too general a term, it should be divided into language and literature. As a subject name I also believe that "English" is too national-centric in that it does not embrace European, American or East Asian writers – the study of their work is equally valid.'

(Year 13 student)

A great many that I spoke to clearly had a sense of the (sometimes bewildering) breadth of the subject, in terms of content,

'Learning about famous playwrights like Shakespeare, grammar work, different writing styles, similes, advertising and the media and essay writing.'

(Year 9 student)

in terms of outcome,

'Everyone needs to learn English because learning to write well in school helps you to get a better job. I also want to be able to understand difficult books because I would like to be able to read anything I choose.'

(Year 8 student)

and in terms of the way it is taught,

'An English teacher should be kind and patient. They should take lessons one step at a time. English teachers shouldn't rush because some students are slower than others and sometimes they can't read and write very well.'

(Year 8 student)

For many of these young people, English was clearly a subject they valued very greatly:

'English lets you be yourself and in your own way express how you feel.'

(Year 10 student)

I do not think the use of the word 'express' here is accidental, because very many of them spoke in a considerably more sophisticated way than I would have expected about the skills they were being, or wanted to be, taught in English. The notion of expressing themselves in a variety of ways – in speaking and listening, reading and writing – came up many times. I find it fascinating that in each of the following comments, what emerges is that the content or nature of texts seems less important to these young people than being given opportunities and strong support for learning how to debate ideas, work in small groups, and use writing both accurately and for a variety of needs. Below are comments in answer to the questions 'What happens in your English lessons?' and 'How would you improve English lessons?':

• What happens in your English lessons?

'Looking at poems and learning about how to write them. Understanding similes and metaphors to make the way we write more interesting. Making sure we can spell difficult words. Learning how to work in groups.'

(Year 8 student)

'Making sense of poetry, letter writing, biographies and autobiographies, finding out about our own tastes in literature, discussing things going on around you and learning how to put forward your own point of view. You are also meant to learn how to write properly. You are not allowed to use slang.'

(Year 10 student)

- How would you improve English lessons?

'I would like more time to study punctuation and grammar – I still don't feel I understand paragraphs – and I want to be able to express myself clearly.'

(Year 9 student)

'I think an English lesson should be where you learn how to write in an interesting way, how to write poetry and perhaps more help with spelling.'

(Year 8 student)

'I would like to see more plays, to learn about the history of English and to have more group discussions debating different points of view.'

(Year 7 student)

'We read our own books, write short stories, poems and have discussions, although the quieter people don't seem to get much out of these debates as they are not usually taking part.'

(Year 8 student)

In each case, these students are talking about far more than the basic language skills I was expecting them to emphasize. They do want to be taught how to spell accurately, certainly, but they also want opportunities for learning how to put forward their *own* point of view, and debate *different* points of view, to *express* themselves clearly, and write in *interesting* ways. The ambitious nature of what they expect from English lessons suggests to me, in fact, that they have actually learnt more about the importance of language than they realize from their English studies.

They have also learnt to be painfully critical, and perceptive, at times:

'I enjoy the media work, particularly studying films – although the film choice of the English Department is not always my choice.'

(Year 10 student)

'Quite a lot gets done though English lessons seem to have more distractions than other lessons because the lessons do not follow as much of a pattern as, say, Science. When we do group work it is easy to have distractions – like when someone starts talking about football or last night's TV.'

(Year 9 student)

'We do some grammar, we watch some films and do topics for no apparent reason. In one lesson a poem was studied and questions answered verbally on a tape recorder. This was supposed to encourage speaking in front of the class and to learn about the purpose of images in a poem. It didn't really work though – the tape recorder encouraged stupidity and name calling.'

(Year 10 student)

I have come to understand, as a result of talking to these young people, just what a wealth of insight into our own practice as teachers the students themselves can provide, if we can only bear to hear some of the things they say. Even a simple comment like 'we seem to do more writing than anything else' (Year 7 student) should be welcomed as a glimpse into the way things look from their side of the desk. The following, slightly more refined version of that complaint about writing certainly did make me think twice about some of the 'desirable' kinds of practice I was being advised to use, both by teachers in school and tutors in the university:

> 'I think most of the stuff we learn will be useful when we leave school but I find having to redraft everything pretty pointless because it takes up so much time.'
>
> (Year 10 student)

Most of all, I learnt from these students how important it was to them that I took my job seriously, and how capable they were of appreciating it when I did so:

> 'I want my English teacher to give me variety, to maintain a balance between being strict and being relaxed. The way I feel about my teacher affects my feelings about the subject – so having a brilliant teacher really helps.'
>
> (Year 9 student)

> 'An English teacher has a degree and is knowledgeable. English teachers talk more and are quite funny.'
>
> (Year 7 student)

> 'The English teacher I respected most created a personal, friendly atmosphere and showed enthusiasm for the subject. They brought what seemed to be the meaningless words of a difficult poem to life.'
>
> (Year 12 student)

As a result both of these conversations with the students, and of my own experiences learning to work with these young people in the classroom, I have come to a number of conclusions about how I see English teaching at this stage of my 'transition from student to teacher'. These I shall present in the next and final section.

A personal perspective on English teaching

In order to get students reading, writing, speaking and listening, and to become active learners, our starting point has to be to create some enthusiasm for the subject of English. Each individual class I have observed has had a different atmosphere, much of which seems to have been generated by the teacher–student relationship. Whilst recognizing that this is not something subject specific, I would argue that by its very nature, English lends itself to a democratic openness in the classroom and that it is an ideal place for stimulating debate rather than the 'teacher relays knowledge, student absorbs', approach. The

English teacher should therefore focus on helping students to talk, to develop their ideas, to argue a case and stand up for themselves. In my teaching practice school, a strong emphasis was placed upon the importance of activities based on student talk, and structured group discussions were a common feature of English lessons. Discussion and debate were treated as valuable exercises in the context of the classroom, and this development of oral skills seemed to be a positive way of giving students strategies for dealing with the outside world.

The first requirement of the English teacher has to be to ensure that students can read and write, to make them literate. Beyond that point, I believe that students should be actively encouraged to read for pleasure and should be provided with an adequate timetable for personal reading. Few classes I observed made this provision beyond Year 7 – a fact which teachers attributed to the limitations imposed upon them by the myriad of other English teaching responsibilities that they were required to perform – SATS eating into Key Stage 3 and the GCSE being the most prominent limitations on the curriculum.

The English teacher must also take responsibility for turning students into competent writers. I believe that the teacher should aim not only to give students a wide range of stimulating tasks that they can engage with, but that they should also provide them with models, conventions and lots of examples rather than assuming a structure will automatically emerge from their writing. It is vital that students' writing should be valued – the classroom displays I have witnessed at my teaching practice school being one way of achieving this. The 'lower set' student who made the low esteem remark, 'our work shouldn't be displayed when it's rubbish' is proof of the need for laudable rather than disposable projects. Special projects which demand extended writing tasks – creative adventures into the unknown; survival on a desert island – were not only met with enthusiasm by Year 7 students but were also a source of motivation in that individuals who had formerly scorned pen and paper appeared eager to use their imagination to maximum effect.

Such assignments effectively answered those often unspoken questions. Why are we doing this? For whom are we supposed to be writing? What am I going to be judged by? It was possible to respond to such work as an interested reader by proposing positive steps for improvement. Long lectures on handwriting – the taunt of the traditionalist – should not to my mind be a teaching priority in an age where word-processing promises to be the dominant form of presentation. Rather than placing the emphasis on surface skills we need to concentrate on ensuring that students' writing is readable, that it makes sense and shows continuity and creativity.

Given that computers are an integral feature of twentieth century living it is to be hoped that students will become information technology (IT) literate. Helping students to achieve IT competency as part of their English studies is the ideal; however in the 'real' world of schools – this was certainly the case at my teaching practice school – where the students' access to computers is quite limited, a lack of commitment to IT training has meant that many teachers are actually less competent in this field than their students.

My professional duty as an English teacher is to provide students with knowledge about language. The underlying assumption of the new National Curriculum orders seems to be that without a fairly comprehensive grounding in vocabulary, grammar and sentence construction no child will be able to communicate lucidly. My personal response is that whilst recognizing the importance of equipping students with a set of basic language rules I believe that it is more appropriate to place grammar in the context of a general lesson rather than in isolation – an approach which often confuses and alienates the students. I have witnessed this grammar-softly approach being employed at Key Stage 3 and 4 levels and in both cases teachers use a common mistake found in students' writing such as paragraphing or misuse of commas, as a focus for a section of the lesson to good effect.

Throughout my experience of teacher practice in school it was clear that Literature was still deemed as being central to the teaching of English and the notion of text was generally confined to books.

In Years 7 and 8 students discover poetry that seeks to please and takes pleasant shape forms or acrostic puzzles; however by Year 10 poetry is a mystery – a detective novel in which the 'teacher did it' by killing the writer. Limited funds result in a predominance of the type of text-book poetry that belonged to the generation of the 1970s. More progressive attempts to broaden students' outlook with multicultural poetry resulted in one student entertaining her classmates with a facetious imitation of patois – which led me to the conclusion that she had somehow missed the point. War poetry is still used to satisfy the boys' perceived lust for blood and attempts to explore more recent conflicts were meaningfully absent, as teachers refused to emerge from the Great War trenches.

Class readers were absorbed through the route of book reviews, diaries and stories designed to provoke character empathy. However, group work and discussion played an important part in the textual journey and resulted in students being able to take charge of taking the words off the page straight to their own experience.

Romeo and Juliet and similar SATs' Shakespearean offerings tended to dominate Year 9 teaching time. Students wrote sonnets, analysed the intricacies of the nurse's role in depth, allocated blame-cakes and became editors of the inevitable 'Globe' teen-suicide report – all for the sake of the SATs.

Teaching the complexities of *Macbeth* demanded that I 'screwed my courage to the sticking-place' as I watched the video, read the text out loud, and carried out activities taken from text books – the ideas which have been handed down the generations of fledgling teachers to be absorbed and reiterated until eventual retirement. The rigours of the unlucky play brought ill portents for those GCSE students whose confidence can be so easily undermined during the early stages of the course. Many students were hesitant to put pen to paper and begin their first essay, and looked for constant reassurance that they were 'getting the right answer' – whilst the rightness of studying the play was never a National Curriculum question. The pressures of exams still dictates there is a definite answer – yet where is the interpretation? Teachers still used GCSE as a form of classroom control, the ultimate threat being 'take note students or you won't pass your exams – this is for your benefit – for your future'.

Apathy and arrogance juxtaposed with flashes of insight characterizes the A-level observation experience where poetry, prose and study of the classics shapes their literary taste, where group study prompts gut responses and where in-depth analysis promotes frantic note-taking. The study of English Literature remains heavily weighted in favour of pre-twentieth century 'greats', as well as Shakespeare of course, and the teacher still sets the agenda whilst allowing students to have some responsibility for interpreting the texts themselves.

The experience of English is constantly being renegotiated yet with all the permanence of classic literature still manages to remain the same. Despite the allegedly progressive nature of many English courses, my own belief – that students be given access to all texts – seems unrealistic. Where is the multi-cultural literature, where is the media work – films are still viewed as a form of light relief – where is the reading for pleasure and more importantly where is the time to ensure that it occurs? Why are texts still given unequal value with the balance weighted heavily in favour of the bard? Literature is still seen as central to the teaching of English and confines the notion of text to book form. My personal belief is that we should give students access to the widest possible range of cultural forms. This means valuing not only the study of classical literature and modern works but also popular culture including newspapers, magazines, radio, television and film. Teachers need to ensure that students learn to overcome their resistance to the past, to recognize that the past is as interesting as the present, that the familiar has value and that there are no such things as sacred texts. Students need to look at all cultural forms critically, to be equal to, not victims of, the text and to be released from the pressure to admire. Such pressure was clearly evident in the response of a Year 10 student to a classic piece of poetry. 'I don't like it,' she said, part apologetic, part defiant.

As a beginning teacher, I started my training with vague notions of what the ideal English lesson should be; images that were shaped by my own experience of school, like the vibrant personality who brought Shakespeare to life rather than the monotone English master who dulled my enthusiasm on a daily basis. Later, having observed English teachers in action, the images become more concrete as I began to deconstruct what takes place in an English classroom: the common teacher concerns such as management, planning, resources, organization and control and the subject specific activities – diaries, ghost stories and the tried, trusted (would it had rusted), 'read around the class'. Delve deeper, and the images crumble under the weight of conflicting forces as to what the English experience should be: the Government view, the global view, tangled academic texts, teachers' beliefs, individual school policy and the vital voice of the silent majority – the English student.

Nowhere between the cover of a single book can the English teacher find a clear comprehensive statement clarifying what English teaching should be. English boundaries cannot be neatly defined, and there appears to be no agreed body of knowledge, so the English teacher can only make choices from what the outside world says and from their inside beliefs which have been – inevitably – shaped by their own experience as students in English classrooms. I think I learnt a very great deal both about how to do the job, and about my own feelings about it, during this part year – but I certainly do not feel that I have yet found the key to English teaching I want to do for the rest of my life, or to the kind of English teacher I want to be.

I do know, though, that English teachers need to be flexible and responsive to change rather than relying on tried and trusted safe lessons – because teaching, like learning, like literacy is a fluid process, a continuous stream you enter into and if you are lucky will carry you through the rest of your life. Without it you are powerless, unable to get work, respect and to meet the demands of the world you are in. Well-educated students can see themselves progressing down the stream of knowledge leaving behind those who simply watch it all pass by them, looking enviously towards something more exciting and bright. The English lesson is a language for life-raft that will begin by keeping students afloat. Gradually ease that support away and students can move downstream as autonomous free thinkers.

8 Summary and implications

This book has not attempted to give instructions in how to teach English. The title *What is English Teaching?* promised something rather more in the way of a philosophical perspective, and that is what I have tried to provide, whilst paying careful attention to real events and recognizing the central importance of what actually happens in classrooms. The aim was to explore the way English has come to be conceptualized, in order to discover what real, structural possibilities lurk below its surface. A great deal is expected of English teaching, and it seems to me that the subject as it is currently constituted cannot yet deliver that, which is why I believe it is so urgent that we locate and make proper use of these possibilities.

In the first two-thirds of the book, I presented my interpretation of what English teaching currently is, and how that came about, all in order to develop an argument about where it does and does not go next. I hope every reader understands what has been going on: I was arguing a case, supported both by a good deal of evidence and by my own 25 years of professional experience; but in the end it is just my argument, just my particular way of seeing things, and it is offered as much in the hope of generating counterarguments as compliance.

But I still believe that it is an important line of argument, even if sometimes it feels like it is about to blow up in my face like bubblegum. I shall summarize it here as clearly as I can, in the knowledge that the simpler I try to make it, the further from reality it is in danger of going. And, having summarized it, I shall then go on and see if I can undermine it with one final twist of perspective.

The way forward

At the heart of this line of argument is my firm belief that literacy teaching and English teaching have become hopelessly tangled up with one another, to the benefit of neither. By literacy, I mean (a) the reading and writing skills that you need in life and (b) the oral skills as well. In other words, 'literacy' is a very broad and very important notion that refers to all the different ways in which we need to be able to use language, as learners, workers, citizens and humans in relationship with other humans. That is a lot of needs and uses, and the more we come to recognize and value the importance for young people of the range of skills and opportunities implied, the more obvious it should be that we are discussing something which stretches *way* beyond the scope of any single school subject area – even that admirably ambitious and unrealistic one called 'English'.

So the first thing I am arguing for – both for the benefit of an improved approach to literacy, and for the benefit of a strong and more coherent English teaching – is that *we cease all pretence that English teaching and literacy teaching are identical.* It has been a long time since that was the case, as the Bullock Report recognized, and as all the subsequent attempts at defining the subject for the National Curriculum so disastrously failed to understand. English teaching and literacy teaching are distinct entities, distinct enterprises and will thrive once viewed as such.

It *is* reasonable, I think, to suggest that everything worthwhile that happens in English contributes to literacy. This is not the same, after all, as saying that everything worthwhile to do with literacy happens in English. English's opportunity to contribute to the improvement of literacy seems to be twofold right now:

1 First, those involved in the subject should firmly insist that English teaching cannot possibly meet all young people's literacy needs. Winning this argument means forcing others to start picking up their equal level of responsibility, which will be a major step forward.
2 Secondly, those involved in English teaching should start to consolidate the more coherent subject that becomes feasible once one abandons the futile effort to cover the fault-line between the specific things that English teaching can do, and the general things it cannot do.

Having won this argument, it then just becomes a matter of turning our attention to how we should divide up the time available to the subject, and what names we should give to those divisions (accepting that we certainly cannot divide up the actual teaching in terms of the language modes of speaking, listening, reading and writing). You will recall, if you have read Chapter 4, that my suggested solution is to operate a straightforward and equal division of the English subject into three areas called (in alphabetical order): knowledge about language, literature study, media study. These are all familiar names, and I am not changing the underlying concepts associated with them, so much as opting for one clear and justifiable assertion about what each should be.

Knowledge about language

This term refers to *explicit* knowledge about what language is in general and what the English language is in particular. Much as the Cox curriculum and

subsequently LINC envisaged it, this involves a broadly sociolinguistic exploration of the relationship between specific and named features of language and
their particular and varying functions in the real world. Such study focuses on
language in society, in order to make young people both more socially and
more linguistically aware.

Literature study

This aspect of English attempts, as it has done for some time, to educate children to read an ever-widening range of texts, in order to learn how to enjoy,
appreciate and talk about what these say and how they say it. The fundamental
aim of such an area of study is to help readers discover what texts are trying
to reveal, in a spirit of good faith. This form of study aims to give young
people access to what different generations and cultures are trying to tell each
other about their lives; it aims to give them access to the excitement or amazement of hearing such things, and thus to enlarge the scope of their lives. This
is already what English teachers do best, and it is hard to imagine anyone
entering the profession without already possessing the basic experience and
skills in such study.

It is crucial to emphasize that the actual texts studied in literature study
and media study need not themselves differ – it is the purposes and methods
of that study which will be different. The point of literature study (as I am
choosing to characterize it) is to seek the pleasures and achievements that *any*
kind of text might contain. There are no particular limitations, therefore, to
the kind of text that might be studied, or to the medium in which it is presented.

Media study

This aspect of English must, on the other hand, try to look at all texts in an
analytical way, in order to learn about the kinds of messages and meanings that
are hidden or encoded within them, and in order to learn how to reveal and
decode those messages. Given the fact that not all texts are benign, that the
world is not always benign, and that it is especially not benign in respect of
those who possess least, this is an immensely important aspect of English (if
one accepts the notion that English is fully concerned with educational and
social justice). This media study is manifestly about making young people as
strong as possible in coping with all kinds of texts, and with the ideologies
encoded in them.

And that is it, really. The deal is that all three areas of English are used both
to teach students about what is going on in various forms of language and
communication, at the same time as providing opportunities for developing
specific literacy/oracy skills. The latter arise, as they do in all subjects, out of
the real demands of the learning that is taking place, and in the English subject

area this involves learning how to use the various modes of language for such purposes as expressing and debating one's own ideas and opinions; exploring one's inner thoughts and feelings; locating, evaluating, synthesizing and interpreting information and evidence. All that and more, because the one thing we can say for sure about English teaching is that it focuses very intensively upon uses of language.

The strategies of English teaching

There is, as I stated at the start of this chapter, one further, fundamental, dimension that needs to be considered in order to answer adequately the question 'What Is English Teaching?'.

Chapters 6 and 7 stated some very important things about the nature of English teaching, not least because they have been written by people who have spent considerably more time during recent months actually doing English teaching than either I or my colleague Peter Benton have. I do not mean to romanticize that – I do not consider that working in classrooms is harder or more heroic than the task of training teachers – but the fact is that the issues that preoccupy both Christine Lawson and Kathy Oxtoby are inevitably different from those of people who, however involved they are in English teaching, do not currently do it on a daily basis. Working every day in the classroom, you tend to think less about what English teaching should be *about*, and to concentrate more on questions of how to make learning happen well.

Currently, it is normal to think of good teaching as requiring that (i) we work out our desired learning outcomes and then (ii) we choose the teaching strategies which have the best chance of achieving those outcomes. This is particularly important in terms of differentiation: first we choose our desired outcomes, and then we adopt a range of flexible strategies which offer various routes through to those desired outcomes for different pupils. I would certainly advocate such an approach myself, but I do think that might make us undervalue one dimension of successful work in English classrooms. I think we need to pay attention to this further dimension, whilst we set about the business of reconceptualizing English for the future – especially if we do so, as we must, on the basis of what English currently is.

When an experienced and currently practising teacher like Christine Lawson talks about the English teaching she wants to provide, and when pupils talk to a sympathetic young teacher about the English teaching they like to experience, they often tend to make no distinction between outcomes and strategies; these often seem to be identical. The principles that Christine Lawson describe involve thinking above all about the quality of how students interact with texts, and with language – in her account, the learning emerges from the way they study things, not what they study – and this seems to be more or less what the pupils also describe, when they talk with such enthusiasm about wanting to learn how to express themselves clearly, how to debate different points of view and wanting to be supported and encouraged by their English teachers in their experiments with language.

These are issues upon which Paul Cooper and Donald McIntyre (1996: 100–1) cast valuable light in reporting recent research into effective teaching and learning (research which focuses in particular upon English teaching in Year 9, in the context of the National Curriculum). They describe at some length how both students and teachers alike 'were deeply concerned with the means by which learning was facilitated in the classroom' and, interestingly, go on to say that 'there was strong agreement between teachers and pupils about the range of most effective teaching strategies and techniques'.

Cooper and McIntyre (1996: 100–1) list a number of the teaching strategies which were seen as valuable aids to learning and understanding (strategies favoured by students are asterisked):

- Teacher making explicit the agenda for the lesson
- Teacher recapping on previous lesson; highlighting continuity between lessons
- Storytelling (by teacher)*
- Reading aloud (by teacher/by pupils)
- Teacher mediation and modification of pupil verbal input to class discussion/ board work
- Oral explanation by teacher, often combined with
    discussion/question answer sessions*
    use of blackboard*
- Blackboard notes and diagrams as aide mémoire
- Use of pictures and other visual stimuli (for exploration/information)*
- Use of 'models' based on pupil work or generated by teacher
- Structure for written work generated and presented by teacher
- Group/pair work (for oral and practical purposes)*
- Drama/role play*
- Printed text/worksheets
- Use of stimuli which relates to pupil pop–culture*

(An additional strategy referred to by pupils only is pupil drawing.)

According to Cooper and McIntyre, the teachers tended to describe themselves as drawing on whatever strategy seemed most appropriate at the time, depending upon the content of the lesson, the mood of the class, and whatever else in the context of a particular lesson might necessitate a particular strategy decision. Students, on the other hand, particularly favoured certain strategies (the asterisked items) in terms of their effectiveness in helping them learn. Students valued strategies such as drama/role play, story-telling and visual stimuli (and also drawing, although the teachers were not themselves too keen on this) because of the way they engaged their attention and imaginations, and in particular they valued opportunities for participating in discussion in the classroom:

From the pupil standpoint, the most valuable shared aspects of these approaches were the opportunities they created for pupils to generate and be exposed to new representations of knowledge and ideas, as well as providing possible confirmation or denial of their own ideas. . . . According to pupils, the most successful class discussions were often those which provided opportunities for autonomous thought and personal expression whilst being carefully directed by the teacher. . . . The fact that pupils were required to articulate their ideas in the discussion phase, also acted as a stimulus for developing and fixing their ideas: '. . . when she was reading, I thought of an idea, and then, when we were asked to do it [i.e. to give their ideas], it sort of really pinged up!'

(Cooper and McIntyre, 1996: 107–8)

These findings are strikingly similar to what emerged from both Christine Lawson's and Kathy Oxtoby's observations: that the really successful and valued teaching strategies were the ones that contributed, not merely to an understanding of particular subject content, but also in themselves constituted what was viewed, especially by the students themselves, as inherently valuable learning about effective language use.

Such a perspective does, I think, slightly alter the argument summarized in the previous section of this chapter: the contribution that English teaching has to make to the general language capacities of students can be found not only in the specific subject content of English (such as the three areas of study outlined in that previous section), but also in the highly effective strategies that English teachers tend to use, ostensibly in order to get that content across. Some of these strategies are obviously also practised by teachers of other subjects, but because of their particular relevance to language-focused learning, these are skills to which English teachers have a special degree of access. The immediate implication, therefore, is that English teachers should seek ways of sharing these strategies with their colleagues who teach other subjects, and who are going to need the support of English teachers in taking on a greater responsibility for improving literacy.

Those with long memories (especially for embarrassment) will perhaps recall the problems that arose in the 'Language across the Curriculum' initiatives that followed the Bullock Report. On the recommendations of that report, headteachers often made the Head of English take on the role of school language coordinator, whose task it was to get everyone thinking about the particular language problems posed by their own subjects. These initiatives had little success, I suspect chiefly because it was not entirely clear what particular aspects of their specialist expertise these English teachers were meant to be sharing. I would suggest that it is the English teaching strategies (located especially in post-Bullock initiatives such as the National Oracy Project and National Writing Project) developed over the intervening years which might well provide the firmest basis for a more sustainable and effective engagement with literacy across the curriculum.

The only negative note to be sounded in this respect is the real fear that the last few years of National Curriculum and SATs development has somewhat knocked the stuffing out of the innovative teaching strategies of English. Certainly, it was evident at the time of John Patten's first attempt to introduce Key Stage 3 English tests that English teachers were forced for a while into abandoning the kind of teaching they valued most. The following accounts (given by teachers at the time) of the impact of the SATs upon their teaching are certainly worrying, if they still hold true:

'A more didactic approach/ More time spent on "bite–size" (superficial) responses to literature (implying a "right" answer)/ Less time to develop individual responses/ Less time to read – think – talk around the subject/ A need to "get through" the whole text, which either means drastically reducing work in other areas or amounts to a superficial reading/ A need for exam preparation – revision time which is not a development of learning.'

(English teacher, School G)

'I've been very conscious of the sort of body of knowledge which has got to be conveyed at speed, you know, from my hands to theirs. [. . . I have done . . .] more leading [. . .] And even more of the straight, you know, standing up in the front of the class and telling them. Which [. . .] I'm not a fan of. It's not a mode of teaching that I think is particularly effective for them [. . .] but I cannot see any other way of doing it in the time.'

(English teacher, School A)

As has been stated on a number of occasions in this book, there is evidence to suggest that the Government did succeed more than we might like to admit in rolling English teaching back to the kinds of traditional method and content that are unlikely to benefit the majority of our pupils. This is discouraging, given that I am not merely arguing here for returning to where we were, but for moving further forward.

The evidence suggests, though, that the subject content and concerns that will serve the real needs of young people as we go careering into the next century do already exist in abundance in the English subject area, if only we can give them the recognition and priority they deserve. And, as this last section has tried to argue, English teachers have additional gifts to offer young people: all those unique practices and strategies of English teaching itself.

Appendix: attitudes to English – questionnaire

Please tick as *appropriate*: ++ = strongly agree; + = agree; ? = no clear response; – = disagree; –– = strongly disagree	++	+	?	–	––
1 It is the primary aim of English to develop a personal response to literature as a way of exploring experience.					
2 The language children bring with them from their home backgrounds should not be criticized, belittled or proscribed.					
3 Good teaching of English at any level should concern itself with educating the sensibility and the emotions.					
4 Our task in English should be to analyse discourses from a political vantage-point.					
5 Critical media literacy is becoming one of the most pressing educational needs of our time.					
6 All literary study reads literary texts in the light of certain values which are related to political beliefs and actions.					
7 As literature recedes from our classrooms, the general level of literacy will continue to fall.					
8 There is no reason for considering the variety called 'standard English' the best for use in all situations.					
9 The study of good literature increasingly gives pupils the vocabulary with which to articulate their own maturing experience.					

Please tick as *appropriate*: ++ = strongly agree; + = agree; ? = no clear response; – = disagree; –– = strongly disagree	++	+	?	–	––
10 In the context of an education system which leaves the majority of people convinced that they're not clever enough to know much about anything, a form of communication such as TV that assumes that they do know, is itself an educational positive.					
11 Far from seeking to control the amount and nature of TV viewing, teachers would be better advised to encourage the growth of more and different ways of using the media.					
12 We must examine texts not so much for what they reveal but for what they conceal.					
13 Literature undoubtedly embodies and transmits the social-aesthetic values of white male bourgeois society.					
14 The attempt to incorporate the study of mass culture into English has resulted in tendencies in the subject towards uncertainty of aim, triviality of content, neglect of the imagination, and concentration upon ephemeral social issues.					
15 Literature, in the sense of a set of works of assured and unalterable value, distinguished by certain shared inherent properties, does not exist.					
16 To say that a piece of language is 'wrong' is merely to make a judgement relative to the social situation in which that language is used.					
17 Reading literature is the cornerstone of our teaching.					
18 The teaching of language is a social and political act.					
19 The social acceptability of a particular language or dialect tells us nothing about its adequacy for communication.					
20 I feel very strongly that a major aspect of my role as a teacher of English is to foster feelings of awareness, sympathy, tolerance and understanding.					

Please tick as *appropriate*: ++ = strongly agree; + = agree; ? = no clear response; − = disagree; −− = strongly disagree	++	+	?	−	−−
21 The best way to teach the language remains what it always was, and that is to expose children to good examples of it.					
22 The attitude of reverence before the text is the one most characteristic of literary interpretation as we practise it, whereas what is needed is a questioning attitude, alert to probe for blind spots and hidden agendas, and highly sceptical.					
23 The literary canon has to be recognized as an artificial construct, fashioned by particular people for particular reasons at a certain time.					
24 If we know what we are doing when we teach poetry, then we shall be secure; the rest of English will follow by implication.					
25 Good poetry undoubtedly does tend to form the soul and character.					
26 Media education is a vital part of any secondary curriculum.					
27 Good English, grammatical and well-spoken, is unfortunately a rarity in our schools today.					
28 Appreciation of literature is not essential: most people get along perfectly well without it, most of the time.					
29 It is not the job of teachers to correct or alter the speech of children who use non-standard varieties of English.					
30 Considering the waste and beastliness of advertising, no-one can contest that opposition to it must be stringent and systematic and very hostile.					
31 We must make a claim for the study of film and TV in their own right, as powerful forces in our culture and significant sources of language and ideas.					
32 Literature should be considered as made up of nothing more or less than a set of arbitrary conventions and structure which we learn to read as literary.					

Please tick as _appropriate_: ++ = strongly agree; + = agree; ? = no clear response; − = disagree; −− = strongly disagree	++	+	?	−	−−
33 There is a right way of using words and constructing sentences, and plenty of wrong ways.					
34 English, more than any other subject, can have an extremely humanizing effect.					
35 Teachers should encourage children to feel positive about their local dialects and to use them creatively in their own writing.					
36 We should drop the illusion that the category 'literature' is objective: anything can be literature, if we choose to regard it as such.					
37 In order to teach the interpretation of a literary text, we must be prepared to teach the cultural and ideological context as well.					
38 The attempt to improve taste, whether about popular culture or literature, is not education but propaganda.					
39 The responsibility of teachers is to the experience of children, their minds, emotions and spirits: it is a matter of knowing the right sort of magic to lead one child from a closed alley of experience to an open one.					
40 It is the responsibility of the school to create an atmosphere of acceptance of all the children in its care and this involves an acceptance of their language.					
41 As English teachers, our business is to enable pupils to develop their reading tastes.					
42 As teachers of English we aim to awaken the sensitivity of our pupils to human emotions.					
43 When it comes to language, we must recapture the concept of the teacher as model − perhaps the only exemplar of the rich resources of the educated and articulate speaker of standard English with whom some children will come into sustained contact throughout their early lives.					
44 Secondary English should provide pupils with an awareness of the crucial relevance of imaginative literature to human experience.					

Please tick as *appropriate*: ++ = strongly agree; + = agree; ? = no clear response; − = disagree; −− = strongly disagree	++	+	?	−	−−
45 The effective English teacher should act as a human bridge between childhood and adulthood.					
46 English teaching should help to prepare children for the accepted values of adult life and write about literature in certain acceptable ways.					
47 To be certificated as proficient in literary studies is merely a matter of being able to talk and write about 'literature' in certain acceptable ways.					
48 The aim of schools must be to provide children with standards against which the offerings of the mass media can appear cut down to size.					
49 There are no 'good' advertisements, only 'effective' ones. In this field, education must always be negative − education against.					
50 Given that mass communications constitute an important area of our experience, we would do well to reflect on their achievements and possibilities − this will not be done if educationists construe their role as one of fighting a rearguard action against the depredations of the media.					
51 Literature consists of all the books − and they are not so many − where moral truth and human passion are touched with a certain largeness and attractiveness of form.					
52 Pupils can enter a fuller, freer life through writing, and by the act of making the kind of moral judgements which are made by writers of fiction, plays and poetry.					
53 We must aim for an English curriculum in which women's writing, black writing and working-class writings will stand strongly alongside the texts of privileged white men.					
54 Good writing is the choice and arrangement of words in such a structure so that the English shall not only be intelligible but beautiful.					
55 The study of English should eventually lead on to the ability to choose good literature rather than bad.					
56 Just as good art can help one to be more fully alive, so bad and indifferent art makes life poorer.					

Bibliography

Apple, M. (1979) *Ideology and Curriculum*, London: Routledge and Kegan Paul.

Ball, S. and Lacey, C. (1994) Subject disciplines as the opportunity for group action: A measured critique of subject sub-cultures. In A.H.P. Woods (ed.) *Classrooms and Staffrooms*, Milton Keynes: Open University Press.

Barnes, D. (1976) *From Communication to Curriculum*, London: Penguin.

Barnes, D., Britton, J. and Rosen, H. (1969) *Language, the Learner and the School*, London: Penguin Education.

Belsey, C. (1980) *Critical Practice*, London: Methuen.

Benton, M. and Fox, G. (1985) *Teaching Literature Nine to Fourteen*, Oxford: Oxford University Press.

Boswell, James (1791) *Life of Johnson*. Standard Authors Edition, 1952 edn., Oxford: Oxford University Press.

Boyson, R. (1975) Maps, chaps and your hundred best books. *Times Educational Supplement* (No. 3150), p. 21.

Brooks, C. St. John (1980) The Transmission of Values in English Teaching. PhD Thesis, University of Bristol.

Brooks, C. St. John (1983) English: a curriculum for personal development. In M.H.A. Hargreaves (ed.) *Curriculum Practice*, Lewes: Falmer Press.

Brunvand, J.H. (1983) *The Vanishing Hitch-hiker: Urban Legends and their Meanings*, London: Pan Books.

Carter, A. (1992) *The Virago Book of Fairy Tales*, London: Virago Press.

Chitty, C. (1989) *Towards a New Education System: The Victory of the New Right?*, Lewes: The Falmer Press.

Cooper, P. and Davies, C. (1993) The impact of National Curriculum assessment arrangements on English teachers' thinking and classroom practice in English secondary schools. *Teaching and Teacher Education* 9 (5/6), 559–70.

Cooper, P. and McIntyre, D. (1996) *Effective Teaching and Learning: Teachers' and Students' Perspectives*, Buckingham: Open University Press.

Coughlan, S. (1993) Junior Points of View, *Times Educational Supplement*, 19 October.

Cross, G. (1995) Credit for borrowing. *Times Educational Supplement*, 19 May.

DES (1975) *A Language for Life*, London: Department of Education and Science.

DES (1985) *The Curriculum from 5 to 16*, London: Department of Education and Science.

DES (1988) *Report of the Committee of Inquiry into the Teaching of English Language*, London: Department of Education and Science.

DES (1989) *English for Ages 5 to 16*, London: Department of Education and Science.

DFE (1995) *English in the National Curriculum*, London: HMSO.

Dickinson, P. (1970) A defence of rubbish. *Children's Literature in Education*, 3, 7–10.

Dixon, J. (1967) *Growth through English*, 1st edn., Oxford: Oxford University Press.

Dyer, R. (1983) Taking popular television seriously. In D. Lusted and P. Drummond (eds) *Popular TV and Schoolchildren*, London: British Film Institute.

Eagleton, T. (1983) *An Introduction to Literary Theory*. Oxford: Basil Blackwell.

Gorman, T.P., White, J., Orchard, L. and Tate, A. (1982) *Language Performance in Schools: Secondary Survey No. 1*, London: HMSO.

Gorman, T.P., White, J., Orchard, L. and Tate, A. (1983) *Language Performance in Schools: Secondary Survey No. 2*, London: HMSO.

Haugen, E. (1972) Dialect, language, nation. In J.B. Pride and J. Holmes (eds) *Sociolinguistics*, London: Penguin Education.

HMI (1984) *English from 5 to 16, Curriculum Matters*, London: HMSO.

HMSO (1963) *The Newsom Report: Half Our Future*, London: HMSO.

Holbrook, D. (1961) *English for Maturity*, Cambridge: Cambridge University Press.

Iles, M. (1995) Boys and Reading: Some Thoughts, *Literacy Today*, 2, March, 5–6.

Knight, C. (1990) *The Making of Tory Education Policy in Post-War Britain 1950–1986*, Lewes: The Falmer Press.

Lawlor, S. (1988) *Correct Core: Simple curricula for English, maths and science. Policy Study*, London: Centre for Policy Study.

Lawson, M. (1995) The story so far is that soap opera has taken over TV. *The Guardian*, 29 May.

Leech, G. and Svartvik, J. (1994) *A Communicative Grammar of English*, 2nd edn., London: Longman.

Lunzer, E. and Gardner, K. (1979) *The Effective Use of Reading*, London: Heinemann Educational.

Marenbon, J. (1987) *English Our English: the new orthodoxy examined. Education Quartet*, London: Centre for Policy Studies.

Masterman, L. (1985) *Teaching the Media*, London: Comedia.

Mathieson, M. (1975) *The Preachers of Culture*, London: George Allen and Unwin.

Moss, G. (1989) *Un/popular Fictions*, London: Virago Press.

Murdock, G. and Phelps, G. (1973) *Mass Media and the Secondary School*, London: Macmillan.

NCC (1992) *National Curriculum English: The Case for Revising the Order*, York: National Curriculum Council.

Neelands, J. (1990) *Structuring Drama Work*, Cambridge: Cambridge University Press.

Orwell, George (1939) Boys' weeklies. In G. Orwell (ed.) *Inside the Whale and other Essays*, London: Penguin.

Pike, C. (1991) Collect call Part II. In T. Pines (ed.) *13 Tales of Horror*, London: Scholastic Children's Books.

Preston, B. (1993) Children spurn books for computers. *The Times*, 31 August.

Pursehouse, Mark (1987) 'Let's have fun with your number one *Sun*': interviews with some *Sun* readers. *Centre for Contemporary Cultural Studies Occasional Paper*, Media Series SP No. 85.

Rawlins, G. and Rich, J. (1985) *Look, Listen and Trust*, London: Macmillan Education.

Sampson, G. (1925) *English for the English*, Cambridge: Cambridge University Press.

Sarland, C. (1991) *Young People Reading: Culture and Response*, Milton Keynes: Open University Press.

Sarland, C. (1995) How not to be frightened by horror. *Literacy Today*, No. 2 (March).

Schutz, A. (1971) 'The Stranger': an essay in social psychology. In B. Cosin, I. Dale, G. Esland and D. Swift (eds) *School and Society: A sociological reader*, London: Routledge and Kegan Paul in association with Open University Press.

Stine, R.L. (1993) *The Hitchhiker; Point Horror*, London: Scholastic Children's Books.

Townsend, J.R. (1990) *Written for Children*, 5th edn., Harmondsworth: Penguin.

Tucker, N. (1994) Bye-bye Biggles, hello Hedgehog. *The Independent*, 31 January.

Warner, M. (1994) *From the Beast to the Blonde*, London: Chatto and Windus.

West, A. (1986) The production of readers. *The English Magazine*, 17, 4–9.

Whitehead, F. *et al.* (1977) *Children and their Books*, London: Macmillan.

Williams, R. (1983) *Writing in Society*, London: Verso Editions.

Young, S. (1993) Time to adjust our sets? *Times Educational Supplement*, 26 March.

Index

ENGLISH TEACHING AND MEDIA EDUCATION

Andrew Goodwyn

The book explores the troubled relationship between English and media education. It places the hostility to the mass media of key figures like Leavis in its historical context, showing how this initial antipathy provided the starting point from which all English teachers began to take the media seriously. By charting the evolution of the media education/English relationship the author argues for siting the majority of media education within the field of English. He makes media theory accessible to English teachers and demonstrates how the developments of the last decade have moved media education away from its previously abstract concerns with purely theoretical matters. He illustrates how media education can be used to develop pupils' enjoyment and critical understanding of all texts within the constraints of the classroom. The National Curriculum has now made media education the official responsibility of all English teachers and the book outlines how to make the most of this opportunity to develop and improve existing good practice in English.

Contents
The relationship between English and media education – The story so far – The media context – English teaching and media theory – Integrating media education – Facing issues and overcoming anxieties – Making it work – Media education, English and the future – Recommended resources – Bibliography – Index.

144pp   0 335 09790 1 (Paperback)

SIMULATIONS IN ENGLISH TEACHING

Paul Bambrough

Simulations allow the exploration of processes and environments which would not otherwise be accessible in the classroom. These might be real world environments or processes, such as a town planning meeting, or fantasy scenarios. Students take on roles and function within these simulated environments to explore both how the world they have entered operates and how they can best function themselves to achieve given objectives in that environment. Simulations are experiential – participants learn by doing. Participants in role feel able to take risks, to fail as well as succeed, and they can look back at and learn from their experience after the event.

Paul Bambrough has applied simulations to the English classroom to allow students to explore language use in social/functional contexts other than those usually experienced, and to enable the exploration of literary texts by allowing students to enter the world of the text.

This book includes sections on simulation design (including a major section on the design of a simulation for working with a text) and using simulations, combining theoretical and practical approaches. No prior knowledge of simulations is assumed, and this is a valuable introduction for all English teachers.

Contents
An introduction to simulations – Designing simulations for English teaching – Designing a simulation – Running the simulation – The debrief – The language experience – Issues of control and reality – References – Index.

112pp   0 335 19151 7 (Paperback)

DESCRIBING LANGUAGE (SECOND EDITION)

David Graddol, Jenny Cheshire and Joan Swann

A student introduction to descriptive linguistics, *Describing Language* is essentially practical in its orientation. It is useful for anyone who wishes to refer to technical literature involving linguistic description, who requires a basic conceptual framework and technical vocabulary with which to discuss language, and who needs to make elementary but principled descriptions and analyses of real data (such as classroom interaction or counselling sessions). Topics covered include phonetics, prosody, word structure, syntax, text and discourse structure, word and utterance meaning, and non-verbal behaviour.

This is a significantly revised, updated and expanded version of the successful first edition. In particular, it uses a new approach to syntax and a broader review of grammar including an accessible introduction to both Chomsky's Universal Grammar and Halliday's Systematic Grammar. It is an invaluable textbook for students across the social sciences.

Contents
Introduction – The nature of language – The sounds of language – Sentence and word structure – Meaning – Writing systems – Face-to-face interaction – Discourse and text – Appendix – References – Index.

256pp   0 335 19315 3 (Paperback)